Crosscurrents / MODERN CRITIQUES

Harry T. Moore, *General Editor*

The Art
of Richard Wright

Edward Margolies

WITH A PREFACE BY

Harry T. Moore

SOUTHERN ILLINOIS UNIVERSITY PRESS
Carbondale and Edwardsville

FEFFER & SIMONS, INC.
London and Amsterdam

Preface

"Now," James Baldwin wrote in 1951, "the most powerful and celebrated statement we have yet had of what it means to be a Negro in America is unquestionably Richard Wright's Native Son." This to a certain extent still holds true, intensified by recent events which have emphasized the dilemma of the blacks. Indeed, Wright's entire career, as man and writer (he died in 1960), has taken on a special new importance in the light of those recent events.

That is why this new book on Wright, by Professor Edward Margolies, is especially welcome now. It deals with Wright not only as an American author of consequence but also as an eloquent participant in the black man's experience. It is an unusually full book, treating not only Wright's imaginative work but also his non-fiction works. The emerging picture is an unusually full one.

And the book is valuably critical; it is not just a beamish discussion of Wright's merits or one of those purely expository studies which do not evaluate and leave the impression that each book is as good as all the others. On the contrary, Mr. Margolies is aware of Wright's defects and points them out convincingly. But on the other hand he shows Wright's merits and in all ways indicates that he is a novelist who continues to be worth our reading time.

Mr. Margolies explores the non-fiction works before turning to the stories and novels, and in the early parts of the book analyzes Wright's thought processes and the general philosophy which underlies the fiction. All this is soundly and sympathetically done.

In the discussion of the fiction, it is good to find Wright's posthumously published (1963) first novel, Lawd Today, treated as one of the author's important books. Professor Margolies notes its literary influences, chiefly avant-garde writers, but indicates that in spite of them it has its own identity.

He also gives full space to Wright's later novels, The Outsider (1953) and The Long Dream (1958), finding them disappointments but with some redeeming elements. Like everyone else dealing with Wright, however, Mr. Margolies takes Native Son (1940) as its author's most significant achievement. The presence of a good deal of propaganda helps weaken Native Son, Mr. Margolies points out, but he also shows that the story has great psychological power. (He deals only briefly with the dramatization by Wright and Paul Green, in which the late Canada Lee gave an overwhelming performance as Bigger Thomas.)

Once again, this is an exceptionally timely book, for it brings back to our attention a man who has a great deal to say to us just now. The judiciously critical tone of the volume deepens its importance.

HARRY T. MOORE

Southern Illinois University
August 16, 1968

Acknowledgments

Although all critical assessments are my own, I should like to name some of the persons whose support and help I have received in writing this study: Doris Alexander, Helen Bokanowski, Michel Fabre, William M. Gibson, Paul Green, Harry Goldberg, Chester Himes, Langston Hughes, Jean Hutson, C. L. R. James, Gunnar Myrdal, Robert Nettleton, John Steinbeck, Oliver Swan, Theodore Ward, Constance Webb, Dr. Frederick Wertham, and Mrs. Louis Wirth.

I should like especially to express thanks to Paul Reynolds and Mrs. Richard Wright who have generously allowed me to look through their extensive files on Richard Wright, and to the staff of the Schomburg Collection of the New York Public Library, who have guided me through their Richard Wright files.

Some of the material originally prepared for the chapter "Revolution: *Native Son*" has appeared in my *Native Sons: A Study of Negro American Authors* (Lippincott, 1968).

Finally, I am indebted to my wife, who has typed this manuscript with care and patience.

E. M.

Contents

The Art of Richard Wright

1

Life and Works

When Richard Wright died on November 28, 1960, *Le Monde* in a lengthy obituary attested to his still powerful European reputation. The response in the United States was scarcely comparable—a few scattered reminiscences followed by a pall of critical silence. Wright had long since been dismissed as a phenomenally successful Negro author of the thirties and forties whose "protest" literature had subsequently become unfashionable. Scarcely any allusion is now made to his literary merit as if by definition one cannot write "sociology" and be aesthetic at the same time.

This is unfortunate because Wright at his best was master of a taut psychological suspense narrative. Even more important, however, are the ways Wright wove his themes of human fear, alienation, guilt, and dread into the overall texture of his work. Some critics may still today stubbornly cling to the notion that Wright was nothing more than a proletarian writer, but it was to these themes that a postwar generation of French writers responded, and not to Wright's Communism—and it is to these themes that future critics must turn primarily if they wish to re-evaluate Wright's work.

Wright's significance in the history of American letters has been shamefully neglected in the last two decades. The reasons are not altogether clear. Perhaps American critics reacting negatively to the fervor of idealism and reform that characterized the New Deal and War years have subconsciously decided to categorize as "immature" authors of that period whom they once favored. Possibly Wright's decision, at the height of his popularity in 1947, to reject America and go to live in Paris has incurred unconscious resentment. Whatever the reasons, a reassessment is in order. Wright not only wrote well but also he paved the way for a new and vigorous generation of Negro authors to deal with subjects that had hitherto been regarded as taboo. Finally, Wright's portraits of oppressed Negroes have made a deep impression on readers the world over.

The images of oppression Wright drew were obviously taken from his own experiences—especially his early years in the South—and it is for this reason that a knowledge of his life is especially helpful. For perhaps no other American writer since Fitzgerald has so intensely relived the themes of his youth in his literature. He was born in 1908 near Natchez, the son of Nathan, a tenant farmer, and a vigorous, strong-willed mother, Ella. Wright's father deserted his family before Richard was six, and Ella was left the sole support of Richard and Leon, his younger brother by two years. Wright chronicles his southern youth and adolescence in his autobiography, *Black Boy* and the grim story he tells scarcely suggests the brilliant career that lay ahead. At four he was a pyromaniac, at six an alcoholic who exhibited disturbing signs of anal eroticisim, and as an adolescent he was involved in theft and a number of petty crimes with other Negro boys. He remained at no one school the entire academic year until the eighth grade (the major part of his formal education in the South) because his mother found it necessary to move herself about from one community to another (in Tennessee, Arkansas, and Mississippi) in search of some kind of livelihood. Often she worked as a cook or as a maid in the homes of white persons, leaving Richard and Leon to cope for themselves. The only other "family" Richard knew were his uncles, aunts, and grandparents—pious Seventh Day Adventists—with whom he lived for a while as an adolescent in Jackson. They sought vainly—often violently—to convert him, but Richard hotly rebelled and after his ninth grade graduation fled to Memphis where he worked at a variety of odd jobs. Here Wright came into his first hostile protracted contact with the white world. He remained in Memphis for a little more than a year and in December, 1927 embarked on a train for Chicago. He was to return to the South only once afterwards on a short visit thirteen years later—but the South or rather his means of psychic survival in the South were to become the major preoccupations of his writings.

Despite the traumas and instability he suffered, Wright's early years were not without their redeeming features. If, for example, he was unable to sink roots in any single southern Negro community because of his mother's constant moves, he was spared, he writes, the abject surrender and apathy that had become so much a part of southern Negro life. Indeed the sense of alienation that is so much a part of Wright's fiction may be traced not simply to the fact that Wright was a Negro living in a hostile racist environment, but that he experienced a profound uneasiness among members of his own family and southern Negroes generally who allowed themselves to become subjugated by a caste system that he had been too footloose to learn. And since Wright had been left so often in his young life to shift for himself, he had come to cherish his solitary freedom however fraught it may have been with peril and upheavals. In short he learned too late the "docility" the southern Negro was presumed to assimilate into his personality, which does not mean that Wright overtly displayed his independence to whites (or Negroes for that matter), but that he quietly knew that southern "reality" did not correspond to his sense of life and so he determined to create his own values out of the hostile or anarchic forces that he found about him.

Hence, Wright's existentialism as it was to be called by a later generation of French authors, was not an intellectually "learned" process (although he had been reading Dostoevsky and Kierkegaard in the thirties) but rather the lived experiences of his growing years. The alienation, the dread, the fear, and the view that one must construct oneself out of the chaos of existence—all elements of his fiction—were for him means of survival. There were, of course, externals he grasped for as well. He was helped in part to survive by the books he voraciously and sometimes surreptitiously read (a literate Negro was often suspect), by the example perhaps of his schoolteacher-relatives and especially his mother who knew the value of an education, and the knowledge that his black grandfather with whom he lived for a while had fought bravely in the Union Army against southern whites. Thus one is forced to observe that despite the extremes of poverty Wright periodically knew in his youth, there were sources of strength in his environment as well.

But Wright obviously did not emerge from the South emotionally unscathed. Since in order to preserve himself he had to deceive both whites and Negroes, he lived not only in constant terror of being found out, but he came to think of all established authority as being in some kind of conspiracy to oppress him, and he carried something of this distrust with him all his life. It explains in part why he later in the thirties joined the American Communist Party, itself a "conspiracy" aligned against what he liked to regard as a conspiratorial conclave of capitalist and imperialist oppressors. It explains in small part, at least, why Wright broke with the Party in 1942, for he felt Party leaders were envious of him for his success. Again later, in Europe, where he spent his last thirteen years, Wright would on occasion suddenly turn against persons and groups with whom he had a great deal in common because he believed they were in league against him. It would almost seem then that the intrigues and counter-intrigues so elaborately devised and worked out by and against the main characters of his fiction fairly accurately mirror the ways Wright often saw himself in relation to the rest of the world.

But, above all, the experiences of his youth made of him the revolutionary he became. Yet paradoxically his revolutionary ardor was born of the desires he most feared in himself. For all his self-imposed isolation and inner discipline, Wright longed to belong to his family, to the Negro community, to the larger community—but not under degrading caste circumstances. And this yearning for community and dignity is everywhere (implicit) in his works. Yet Wright was all his life convinced that these aims, however desirable, are unattainable under capitalism, and even after his "god" the Communist Party failed him in 1942, he remained a Marxist of sorts, believing in the necessity of a socialist upheaval of society. But with the passing of the postwar years, he came to despair of the West resuscitating itself in the image of its best ideals, and during the last decade of his life he wrote that perhaps the most hopeful signs for the future lay in the newly emerging nations of Africa and Asia. In supporting color nationalism, Wright was in one sense returning to views he had long before held as a Communist in the early Depression years. Wright's nationalism at that time was in part a kind of unconscious counter-racism, in part derived from the Communist Party platform, calling for the establishment of a separate Negro state in the South. All told though, Wright's racial feelings even at this early period appear to have run deeper than his ideology. On the three occasions he treats white Communists in his proletarian fiction, they are at best ignorant of what the Negro really feels —and at worst villainous.

The roots of Wright's color nationalism lay ob-

viously in his southern upbringing, but since Wright
—judging from what he says about himself in his autobiography—could not easily identify with other southern Negroes, his feelings were more mixed than he
imagined. Much of his antagonism appears directed
against white women who were presumed to require
the protection of Jim Crow laws against Negro sexuality. (Wright's grandmother, incidentally, a formida-
ble woman who sometimes beat him could easily have
"passed" as white.) There is ambiguity in Wright's
treatment of white or fair-complexioned women. Now
and then they are desired as status symbols or because
they are supposedly beyond reach; on the other hand
there are occasions when Wright's protagonists violently attack them. Sometimes white women in
Wright's fiction find Negro males attractive because
of the mythos about their virility. Interestingly, Negro
men and Negro women do not fare much better than
interracial couples. Clearly the reasons are that poverty, unemployment, and caste practices generally
have deprived Wright's Negro men of their sense of
dignity and manhood.

Although Wright's departure for the city liberated
him from southern racial violence, the very absence of
explicit caste restraints exacerbated his anxieties. But
his already-achieved self-willed withdrawal from others probably enabled him to cope with the depersonal-
ized bustle of the city more effectively than other
southern migrants for whom the sundering of traditional folk-communal ties represented a terrifying experience. In the forties he would write about these
people and their city-born offspring who would feel as
alienated from their families and environment as the
young Wright had felt in Mississippi. But however
dreary and confining ghetto life may have been,
Wright found it in the long run beneficial. Here at
least there existed no visible curbs on political and
intellectual interchange. And Wright arrived at a time
when Negro nationalism (Marcus Garvey's Back-to-

Africa movement) and the new Negro literary movement (the Harlem Renaissance) were still very much topics of current interest in northern Negro urban communities. He now read voraciously (Mencken, Dreiser, and Gertrude Stein were among his first loves) and worked for several years at a variety of odd jobs. One of the best of these—was at the Post Office where in 1932 a white companion, learning of Wright's interest in literature, introduced him to the Chicago John Reed Club. Thus was Wright's literary career first truly launched although he had already produced one short story in the South and another for *Abbots Monthly* in 1930. But Wright found the atmosphere of the John Reed Club especially stimulating for working-class artists and started producing proletarian poems, a number of which saw publication over a five year period (1934–1939) in *New Masses* and other left wing periodicals.

With the onset of the Depression—especially bitter for Negroes—he was persuaded to Marxism and joined the Communist Party sometime in late 1933. He remained a relatively active member for the next seven or eight years although he was undoubtedly always somewhat restive under Party discipline. His first novel *Lawd Today*, written perhaps in 1936, he did not attempt to publish out of deference to Party aestheticians who might not have liked Wright's unsympathetic treatment of his lower middle-class Negro protagonist. But the mere fact that Wright could have written such a book at the time he did indicates that Wright was not wholly commited to the Party viewpoint. And he was meanwhile coming into contact with wider intellectual currents. In 1935 he had begun working for the Illinois Federal Writers Project which required of him some knowledge of the research techniques of the historian and sociologist.

In 1937, he obtained a position on the *Daily Worker* and moved to New York. The following year he worked on the New York Federal Writers Project contributing an essay on Harlem which remains today a well-written, informative scholarly piece. In 1938 after having won a cash award from *Story Magazine*, Wright published four lengthy short stories with *Harpers* under the title *Uncle Tom's Children*. (A fifth one was added in the 1940 edition.) Two years later *Native Son* electrified the reading public and Wright and his novel became objects of controversy.

Most of the charges and counter-charges regarding *Native Son* lay outside the realm of aesthetics. Wright's most obvious thesis was that Bigger Thomas, a sullen, resentful, adolescent murderer was a product of the slum ghetto environment that brutalized him, although, as we shall see, the implications of the novel lay beyond the sociological. Many readers objected, among them a large number of Negroes, that Wright himself was an example of someone who transcended his environment—and they expressed themselves grieved that he had portrayed in Bigger an image of the Negro that enlightened whites and Negroes had long been trying to erase from the public mind. What shocked readers most perhaps (beyond the fact that one of the persons Bigger murders was a friendly white girl) was the seething hate Bigger is made to feel toward all whites. In heated responses to his critics, Wright insisted that he had known such persons as Bigger all his life and that if they did not commit murder, it was not because murder was not in their hearts. Meanwhile Party officials, although publicly praising the work, privately protested to Wright that it contained ideological errors. But regardless of the merits of the controversy, the sensational subject matter of the novel swelled its sales and Wright discovered himself suddenly catapulted into the role of "spokesman." Early the following year, 1941, saw the Orson Welles Mercury Theater Broadway production of the play *Native Son* that Wright had written with Paul Green the previous summer. Later in 1941 Viking published the Negro folk history, *12 Million Black*

Voices, that Wright had produced in collaboration with the photographer, Edwin Rosskam. Shortly thereafter Wright announced his break with the Communist Party.

Besides his personal feelings about Party leaders, Wright's uneasiness with Communism was occasioned by intellectual differences as well, some of which were becoming more apparent in his works. The decision to leave the Party was especially difficult because the Party had for a long time provided him with the dignity and community Wright had always longed for as a youth. And now he was made to face again a dread, alien, designless world, a world in which he would have to rediscover himself—by himself. He was undoubtedly helped in this process by the friendships he had formed with University of Chicago sociologists Louis Wirth and Robert Park—and later by the New York psychiatrist, Frederick Wertham. All three helped redirect his reading and carried on lengthy discussions with him. Their influence may be discerned as early as 12 *Million Black Voices* and became progressively more pronounced in the two versions of Wright's novella *The Man Who Lived Underground* (1941, 1943), his introductory essay to Horace Cayton and St. Clair Drake's study of the Chicago Negro, *Black Metropolis* (1944), and his autobiography *Black Boy* (1945). In most of these works Wright's orientation strikes one as being more psychological and metaphysical than Marxist—although as has been indicated earlier Wright's severance with the Party does not imply a total disillusionment with Marxism.

Wright was of course in this period especially interested in the migrant southern Negro in the industrial North and his city-born children. (Even Wright's last unpublished chapter of the original manuscript of *Black Boy* relates partially to this subject.) And generally in his works of the forties, Wright focuses on the existential agony of migrant Negroes recently fled from the feudal South who attempt to learn the unwritten, elusive and contradictory ways of the city. Yet despite their traumas, the city, by its very nature, opens up to them the possibilities of freedom. In several of his pieces Wright warns that subsequent generations of urban-born Negroes would no longer submit to inferior status or exclusion—a prognosis of ghetto upheavals that now wrack American cities.

If Wright was, as we have seen, indebted to sources other than Marx for his analysis of Negro American life, it must also be conceded that the views he chose to express correspond to his own personal experiences. Thus when he left permanently for Europe in 1947, he was gloomy about America. There was more freedom, he told a reporter, in one square foot of Paris than in all of the United States. He suggested to friends more quietly that he would not want to bring up his children under humiliating racial conditions. France did indeed appear to strike Wright as an ideal place to live and work. The preceding year when he had been invited to Paris by his new-found literary admirer, Gertrude Stein, he had been festively welcomed and honored by a number of French authors who seemed to regard him as a kindred spirit. But Wright's literary output in Europe—with the exception of the more than two thousand hakku poems (unpublished) he wrote during the last year of his life—was not high. He produced only three more novels, all of them with American settings (*The Outsider*, 1953; *Savage Holiday*, 1954; *The Long Dream*, 1958), which in the main reiterate his preoccupations of the thirties and the forties. Some of his shorter fiction gathered in the posthumous volume *Eight Men* (1961), and other miscellany as yet unpublished indicate he was moving toward an international theme before his death.

But if Wright's purely creative endeavor suffered somewhat from his move to France, his political and historical vision deepened. Shortly after his arrival in Paris he immersed himself in the problems of colonialism and along with Gide, Camus, Sartre, and a host of French and French-African writers helped to found, in 1948, the still flourishing *Présence Africaine*, a journal devoted largely to the arts and politics of Africa. And in the following decade he was instrumental in promoting the several African writers' conferences that met in Paris and Rome. Finally, during the first five years of the fifties he delivered a series of lectures throughout Europe on racial and colonial issues—and occasionally a lecture on Negro American literature. (These he gathered in the collection, *White Man Listen!*, 1957.) Yet despite all these activities, Wright, always a generous person, maintained an open door to the variety of Negro American and European and African writers and intellectuals who trekked often from abroad to visit him.

One of Wright's principal means of support in the fifties was the publication of his travel books. In 1953 he visited the Gold Coast and witnessed there the initial birth throes of Ghana (*Black Power*, 1954). Two years later he attended the first Afro-Asian summit conference in Bandung, Indonesia (*The Color Curtain*, 1956). In addition, he recorded his impressions of the "oppressed" Spanish people nearly twenty years after their Civil War (*Pagan Spain*, 1956). But again, as in his nonfiction of the forties, although Wright read deeply around the subjects about which he would write, a number of his conclusions appear to be drawn from his own special Negro American experience. (He had long alluded to Negroes as a people colonized and exploited by a master civilization.) In his works of the fifties, he warns the new countries of Africa and Asia to be wary of attempts of Caucasian nations to re-exploit them. The colored leaders of the new nations, he writes, are psychological outsiders (not unlike the way Wright had elsewhere described himself) who have had to create their nations and themselves out of forces hostile or indifferent to their being. Finally, he frequently attempts to probe the psychology of the oppressors as well as the oppressed in his books.

In the chapters that follow I shall attempt to examine at some length the development of Wright's art and ideas in his major published works. But before doing so perhaps a word more need be said. Wright was important obviously for his influence and for what he achieved in American letters. But perhaps even more significant was the man himself. For in a peculiar sense he was himself the embodiment of the changes in Negro life he often wrote about—as he himself emerged from the structured, rural South to the urban industrialized North and hence to the arena of international affairs. For this reason alone, an examination of his writings may yield a richer response than one might at first suppose.

2

The Fractured Personality
Black Boy; 12 *Million Black Voices*

In general, Wright's nonfiction takes one of two directions. The first concerns itself with the devastating emotional impact of centuries of exploitation on its individual victims. The second is the overall cultural characteristics of oppressed peoples. The first is largely psychological; the second socio-anthropological. Obviously no such absolute division obtains since it is impossible to discuss one without making reference to the other, but for purposes of analysis it may be said that Wright lays greater or lesser stress on one or the other of these issues in each of his works of nonfiction. *Black Boy* (1945), Wright's autobiography of his Southern years, serves perhaps as the best point of reference from which to make an examination of his ideas, since, as we have seen, Wright generalizes from his own experiences certain conclusions about the problems of minorities everywhere.

In producing his autobiography, Wright was beset by certain kinds of moral problems which ordinarily do not confound other authors. How much of the "whole truth" should he record? Would anything he transcribed tend to hurt the cause of the people whom he was championing? Moreover, in his role of "spokesman," would he be guilty of artistic or moral transgression if he were to fictionalize some of the events in his life in order to make a larger point—to tell a larger truth? (On the second of these problems Wright did indeed suppress certain facts which might have made some aspects of his upbringing appear less sinister. He does not, for example, tell of his friendship with the sons of a college president in Jackson nor does he allude to the fact that his mother, like several of his aunts and uncles, occasionally taught school. Such information might imply middle-class elements in his background, thereby possibly endangering Wright's peasant and proletarian credentials.) The reader, in turn, in evaluating *Black Boy*, is confronted by the same kind of difficulties. How much of *Black Boy* is true autobiography; that is to say, how well does Wright convey his true personality and character against the context of an environment which one feels may not be quite literally accurate—and how much of *Black Boy* is to be read in terms of an essay in race relationships in the South? Must the reader in judging *Black Boy* have at his disposal two sets of standards—and if he does, how is he to know when to apply either? Possibly the problems presented by *Black Boy* are insoluble since the environment in which *Black Boy* operates is so alien to the average reader that it is almost essential for Wright to hammer home in little digressive essays the mores of the caste system so that *Black Boy's* psychology and behavior may be better understood. As a result, its authority as autobiography is reduced—Wright frequently appears to stand aside and analyze himself rather than allow the reader to make inferences about his character and emotions from his actions—and its strength as sociology seems somewhat adulterated by the incursions of the narrative. Yet, despite these failures—or possibly because of them—the impact of the book is considerable and this perhaps is Wright's artistic triumph.

A reading of *Black Boy* in some respects resembles a movie documentary. There is the voice of the narrator —Wright's own voice—which announces and interprets the action; there is the skillful manipulation of the camera—Wright's interspersed and lyrical passages —which focuses on and picks up the nuances of the natural beauty of the southern landscape and drowsy violence of its atmosphere. There are the occasional bits of dialogue as Wright himself confronts members of his family and his white employers. And finally, there is the didactic-belligerent-defensive tone of the whole piece, which one associates with certain documentaries whose aim is to arouse in their audience the urge to act. The book is structured episodically, highlighting certain events in Wright's life from the age of four up through his adolescence when he left the South.

Wright's purposes in writing the book were threefold. He was first concerned with describing his own intellectual and emotional growth—and explaining how it was that he did not fall into the stereotyped pattern of the behavioral responses of the southern Negro community. He was also interested in showing how the caste system literally blights the lives of the Negro minority. And finally, he wanted to indicate how the system of race relations in the South brutalizes and dehumanizes the lives of the white ruling class. Insofar as any of these purposes is fulfilled, the first—relating to his psychological development—succeeds better than the others—perhaps more than Wright himself knew. The reason lies in the fact that Wright's account of his experience allows his readers to induce aspects of his character of which Wright himself may not have been aware despite his propensity to argue and explain. To be sure, the ways in which Wright discovered himself alienated from his family and other Negroes are convincingly and dramatically portrayed. But there are significant omissions in his discussion of other areas of his emotional life. There is, for example, scarcely any mention of sexual attraction or physical longings in adolescent years. Sex is generally conceived of in terms of violence (the dangers inherent in relationships with white prostitutes); bravado (adolescent boys speaking of their prowess); adultery (his father's abandonment of his wife for another woman); obscenities (which Wright learned at the age of six); or condescension and rejection (Wright's fending off the daughter of his landlady in Memphis because she was incapable of understanding the depths of his sensibilities). The only occasion on which Wright alludes to his physical desires is when he was twelve and yearned for the elder's wife in his grandmother's church.

More important perhaps are Wright's attitudes toward other Negroes. Although Wright's outsider role as an author does not require him to identify with them completely, what is astonishing is how frequently he rejects them! Scarcely anywhere are they mentioned favorably, although along with his mother, they are once or twice objects of compassion. More frequently they are "petty," "shallow," "insensitive," "unstable," and lacking in kindness, loyalty, or memory. Nor is Wright's portraiture of individual Negroes any the more flattering. They are stereotyped and one-dimensional. They exist only insofar as Wright reacts to them—and serve only to frustrate him in his ambitions to express himself, and to discover the meaning of "meaningless suffering." Only his mother and grandmother possess a vitality peculiarly their own. Given Wright's self-willed isolation, this is understandable. How would he have been able to probe their complexities, their sufferings, their warmth, their laughter, their terrors, their dreams? And was a southern Negro culture that produced a Leadbelly, a Bessie Smith, and the blues really so barren of meaning and human insight? (Oddly, Wright was far more capable of exercising sympathetic insights into the character of southern Negroes in his short stories possibly because he was not now immediately and directly involved in their lives.) And, of course, Wright's description of southern whites is totally savage. They are cruel, violent, and obsessed with hatred and contempt for Negroes. They go out of their way to humiliate and debase any expression of the Negro's humanity. It would perhaps be too much to expect Wright to understand them in terms of their guilt and their frustrations—yet their monstrousness borders on the unreal.

How then does the autobiography achieve its effects? Wright's theme is freedom and he skillfully arranges and selects his scenes in such a way that he is constantly made to appear the innocent victim of the tyranny of his family or the outrages of the white community. Nowhere in the book are Wright's actions and thoughts reprehensible. The characteristics he attributes to himself are in marked contrast to those of other characters in the book. He is "realistic," "creative," "passionate," "courageous," and maladjusted because he refuses to conform. Insofar as the reader identifies Wright's cause with the cause of Negro freedom, it is because Wright is a Negro—but a careful reading of the book indicates that Wright expressly divorces himself from other Negroes. Indeed rarely in the book does Wright reveal concern for Negroes as a group. Hence Wright traps the reader in a stereotyped response—the same stereotyped response that Wright is fighting throughout the book: that is, that all Negroes are alike and react alike.

Sometimes, Wright resorts to large infusions of pseudo-poetic nostalgia which are intended to offset the intolerable tension of the story he is telling:

> There was the drenching hospitality in the pervading smell of sweet magnolias. There was the aura of limitless freedom distilled from the rolling sweep of tall green grass swaying and glinting in the wind and sun.[1]

But his most effective stylistic device is his use of dialogue. Here he dramatically transports the reader into the situation he is experiencing—and leaves the reader no alternative but to identify with Black Boy. Wright has a keen ear and accurately reproduces the rhythms and speech patterns of any conversation he is recording. Ordinarily Black Boy's responses in these colloquies are laconic and defensive. He is fighting for his life with every breath he takes.

"Do you want this job?" the woman asked.
"Yes, Ma'am," I said, afraid to trust my own judgment.
"Now, boy, I want to ask you one question and I want you to tell me the truth," she said.
"Yes, ma'am," I said, all attention.
"Do you steal?" she asked me seriously.
I burst into a laugh and then checked myself.
"What's so damn funny about that?" she asked.
"Lady, if I was a thief, I'd never tell anybody."
"What do you mean?" she blazed with a red face.
I had made a mistake during my first five minutes in the white world. I hung my head.[2]

In these ways Wright artfully contrives the case against Negro oppression—by focusing attention on himself who, paradoxically, escaped its worst ravages.

Wright's earlier book, 12 *Million Black Voices* (1941), anticipates *Black Boy* in several respects. While it purports to be a folk history of the Negro people, it contains in essence Wright's personal reaction to his southern environment and the shocks he felt on first coming into contact with urban life. Moreover, the views he later developed in his speech before the 1956 African Writers' Congress in Paris ("Tradition and Industrialization")[3] are announced here for the first time. This is especially interesting since Wright at the time he produced the book was still an active member of the Communist Party—and although his outlook here regarding the "conscious sphere of history" into which he says the Negro proletariat is moving is decidedly Marxist, he is more convincing when he describes the disintegration of Negro folk culture and the "atomization" of the Negro personality—problems which Wright himself experienced keenly in his Chicago years. The principal difference in the tone of the books is that Wright in 12 *Million Black Voices* identifies with the Negro masses—the history is related in the first person plural—in a kind of "the people are the salt of the earth" manner whereas in his autobiography they are (unconsciously) the enemy.

But despite Wright's intentions 12 *Million Black Voices* is something more than a folk history. It is an account which attempts to trace the political, social, and economic destinies of American Negroes from the inception of slavery in 1619 up until the present time (1941). Wright's principal thesis is that the Negro's experience—from the time he was snatched away from his family-centered tribal society to the time he arrived in the highly industrialized cities of the North—represents in miniature the American experience—indeed the larger experience of Western civilization. If America's Negroes perish, then America will perish because the Negro experience is what America is. Indeed the Negro is a mirror of the living past since "our memories go back through our black folk of today, through the recollection of our black grandparents, to the time when none of us, black or white, lived in this fertile land."

But Wright sometimes contradicts himself. No one obviously would deny that the successive stages of acculturation that the Negro has undergone over the past three hundred years have not, in the main, mirrored the same experience whites have undergone over a much longer period of time. Yet Wright's view that the memory of these different modes of life lives on in the consciousness of "black folk" is a bit of romantic legerdemain. The tragedy of the American Negro, as Wright notes elsewhere in the book, is that centuries of chattel slavery, and economic and social discrimination have stripped him of traditions, and memories, and that the fragile folk culture that he has precariously built up from plantation days is rapidly disappearing in the bustle of urban life. Thus the sense of the past which is so essential a support of the ego is lacking, and the Negro is left an empty husk of identity.

One of Wright's themes in 12 *Million Black Voices* is the Negro's long march toward freedom. The historical processes of the West, Wright feels, have evolved in the direction of freedom for the great mass of humanity—but freedom here is not simply defined as a political or social condition but the triumph of Western rationality and science over irrational fears and superstitions—in a word, religion. (There is a strong anti-religious bias in practically all of Wright's works. In the fifties he would regard African religions as one of the main stumbling blocks to the progress of the newly emerging colonial countries.) Ironically, the subjugation of the black man was the necessary ingredient which catalyzed these historical processes—because Negro labor was essential to create the wealth through which the West came to flower. But the Negro has now become a Westerner in spirit as well as in fact, and clamors for his freedom along with other dispossessed Americans. "We learn the ways of life of the Western world. Behind our pushing is the force of life itself as strong in black men as in white, as emergent in us as those who contrive to keep us down." [4]

Although Wright stresses the psychological devastation Negroes have suffered in the West, he writes as well as if there were something romantically ennobling about their poverty. Occasionally a kind of Marxist lyricism creeps into his prose.

> So, living by folk tradition, possessing but a few rights which others respect, we are unable to establish our family groups upon a basis of property ownership. For the most part our delicate families are held together by love, sympathy, pity, and the goading knowledge that we must work together to make a crop. [5]

There are, he says, three classes of people who stand above him and oppress him: dispossessed poor southern whites and northern industrial workers who fear for their jobs; "Lords of the Land," southern plantation owners; and "Bosses of the Building," urban property owners, industrialists, and bankers. The metaphor Wright most constantly uses in describing this struggle is the metaphor of warfare and violence. When a white man decides to sell his home to a black buyer, the "black family 'invades' a white neighborhood and is greeted by violence. . . . Grudgingly the white population fall back street by street . . . until the warfare begins again." [6] Negro "scabs" fight mobs of white workers in the city streets. "After scores of such battles . . . we black folk gain a precarious foothold in the industries of the North. . . . Life for us is constant warfare and . . . we live hard, like soldiers . . . our kitchenettes comprise our barracks; the color of our skin constitutes our uniforms; the streets of our cities are our trenches; a job is a pill-box to be captured and held. . . . The Bosses of the Buildings are the generals who decree the advance or retreat." [7] The class struggle determines the course of world history. Even where Negroes are not immediately involved, they are made the pawns of contending economic forces over which they have no control. The American Civil War, for example, is a conflict between two kinds of capitalism—symbolized by the Lords of the Land and the Bosses of the Buildings. Humanitarian considerations for the slaves were only incidental. "We were freed because of a gnawing of some obscure sense of guilt, because of a cloudy premonition of impending disaster, because of a soil becoming rapidly impoverished, because of the hunger for fresh land, because of the new logic of life that came in the wake of clanking machines—it was all these things, and not the strength of moral ideals alone." [8]

Wright's Marxist analysis perhaps makes simplified history. But 12 *Million Black Voices* is intended not as a scholarly study but rather as a kind of prose-poem account of the lives of simple folk in their own voice. As such, it does not always succeed. Too often Wright is tempted to step outside his own role of narrator and interpret events in a way which his simple "black folk" would be unable to do. Moreover, Edwin Rosskam's photographs, which comprise half the space of the book, must to some extent have determined the contents of the book. The vocabulary is surely not the vocabulary of the folk, nor are the pace and cadences of Wright's sometimes inflated rhetoric always appropriate to his subject. Yet for all that, the book does manage to cover an amazingly large amount of material in a relatively brief span of pages. Relevant economic data is given; the Negro's social position in the deep South and the cities of the North is brilliantly etched; the psychology of the Negro peasant and urban dwellers (making some reservations for Wright's romanticism) is lucidly conveyed; the photographs for the most part adequately, often vividly and dramatically, complement the text as do the fragments of doggerel verse and songs. Further, Wright includes sociological data such as Negro church services, leisure activities, and family life at appropriate moments. Each of the four chapters into which the book is divided is designed to represent the point of view of a new generation of Negroes. But Wright's Marxist voice frequently intrudes—and there is considerable shuttling back and forth in time as Wright attempts to explain the meaning of events.

Ironically, Wright is often at his best when he loses sight of his political purposes and celebrates the American landscape in almost mystical poetic terms. He has a Whitmanesque love of place names and names of things, and he possesses the ability to evoke sights, sounds and smells:

> The land we till is beautiful, with red and black and brown clay, with fresh and hungry smells, with pine trees and palm trees, with rolling hills and swampy delta—an unbelievably fertile land, bounded on the North by the states of Pennsylvania, Ohio, Illinois and Indiana, on the South by the Gulf of Mexico, on the West by the Mississippi River, and on the East by the Atlantic Ocean.[9]

There is something in this work that suggests Sandburg's *The People, Yes* and perhaps Masters' *Spoon River Anthology* (two authors whom Wright had read as a boy). But *12 Million Black Voices* is far more ambitious than either and therein lie its principal weaknesses. For Wright attempts to do too much and thus does too little. Is it history, is it sociology, is it literature, is it propaganda? Wright clearly intended his book to be all of these—and it is not quite any of these. Yet his effort need not be gainsaid; *12 Million Black Voices* represents a mind burgeoning with politics, philosophy, poetry, and social conscience that has not quite coalesced into an orderly pattern.

3

The Fractured Personality
Black Power; Pagan Spain

In the summer of 1953, Wright undertook a journey through the primitive country of the British West African colony of the Gold Coast. He had, a few months earlier, completed a first draft of a new novel, *Savage Holiday*, and now felt free to give rein to his African interests. The trip was suggested to him by Mrs. George Padmore,[1] who had been visiting the Wrights in Paris in the spring of 1953. The Gold Coast was, at the time Wright decided to make the journey, in the throes of wresting full political independence from Great Britain under Kwame Nkrumah's Convention People's Party, and Wright had arranged through Mrs. Padmore's husband in London to meet the Prime Minister and several of his political aides. Wright sailed from Liverpool at his own expense and arrived at the coast port city of Takoradi on June 16, where he was met by one of Mr. Nkrumah's friends and escorted on a government bus to the capital, Accra, one hundred and seventy miles to the east. In Accra Wright met Prime Minister Nkrumah several times and on two or three occasions accompanied him on political rallies. On one of these occasions he delivered a speech from the same platform as the Prime Minister in which he wished the people of the Gold Coast success in their drive for independence. In addition to his political investigations, Wright trudged the streets and compounds of Accra and surrounding villages gleaning impressions of the teeming and exotic life he saw about him. He interviewed as many native Africans as he could, spoke to Nkrumah's political opposition among the black intellectuals, and even struck up cursory relationships with white colonial officials and businessmen. The following month Wright took a motor trip through the thick jungle Ashanti country to Kumasi and returned by way of Takoradi. In each of the villages he visited, Wright managed to obtain interviews with tribal chiefs and white British colonial officials and civilians who were serving the back country in various capacities. He witnessed firsthand the flourishing gold-mining and timber industries, and at the same time made careful observations of the native laborers who worked at these industries. On September 2, Wright departed from the Gold Coast to return to Paris; he did not know it at the time, but he had contracted an intestinal amoeba during his travels which would be a contributory cause of his death seven years later.

Black Power is a pot-pourri of the impressions Wright gained on his trip through Africa. But it is more than that; it is an extensive essay of personal journalism in which the writer draws certain conclusions about the culture, the people, and the political, social, and economic problems facing the first African nation to achieve political independence after the second World War. It contains Wright's personal suggestions to Nkrumah as to how these problems may be resolved. And finally, in a profound way, it is a book about Wright himself. In a short introduction which he calls "Apropos Prepossessions," Wright states that the aim of the book is to pose anew the question whether the West will again abandon its standards of justice, ideals and traditions in dealing with its nonwhite subject peoples. If this happens, the colored colonial areas may indeed fall prey to Communism, since "Communist strength is predicated upon Western stupidity, moral obtuseness [and] foolish racial jealousies." [2] But if Wright's purpose in writing the book was to challenge the West, his reasons for going to Africa, in the first place, were extremely personal.

When Dorothy Padmore suggested he visit Africa, Wright was once more confronted with the problem of identity which had been plaguing him ever since his Mississippi boyhood. What is a Negro? What is an African? Wright had been writing since his Chicago days that the Negro was a psychological and sociological phenomenon, a bundle of emotional and intellectual attitudes created by a warped and terrified white world. Remove the strictures that prohibit the Negro from expressing his humanity and he would be the same as anyone else. Now he would be able to test his assumptions against firsthand experience. The feelings Wright underwent as a result of his opportunity were far from simple. Were there indeed "racial qualities" which native Africans might recognize in him? How would he feel about a people whose ancestors sold his ancestors into slavery? How would *they* feel about him? Was he African? "My mind and feelings were racing along a hidden track," he wrote. Did there exist some "definite ancestral reality that would unlock the hearts and feelings of the Africans whom I'd meet?" [3] His self-doubts do serve, to a degree, to cast doubt on some of the judgments he makes throughout the trip. Yet as in *Pagan Spain*, one wonders whether it is not possible that Wright's special experiences as a member of a despised ethnic group did not, for that reason, better equip him to perceive the realities of oppression.

Black Power makes no pretense to outsider objectivity. The problem of "race" confronts Wright wherever he goes. He wonders about "African survivals" in his own personality and in the identity of Negroes elsewhere. There is the strange shuffling gait of African dancers in Accra which reminds him of similar movements he had witnessed at Holy Roller Tabernacles and storefront churches in the United States. He sees some function now for nappy hair as he observes school children and clerks stick their pencils between the kinks so as not to lose them. He puzzles over other "items of similarity . . . that laughter that bent the knee and turned the head (as if in embarrassment!); that queer shuffling of the feet when one was satisfied or in agreement; that inexplicable, almost sullen silence that came from disagreement or opposition." [4] He reacts to Christian missionary efforts in the same manner as he reacted to his grandmother's attempts to convert him. Just as his grandmother sometimes tried to deprive him of his freedom as a means of deriving satisfaction for her own neurotic needs, so were the missionaries endeavoring to subjugate and exploit Africans. (Yet, paradoxically, he is even more appalled at the practices and beliefs of the native pagan religion.) His suspicions of the white West's attitude toward African independence are grounded in his own ambivalent feelings toward whites. On the one hand, he is a Westerner—and admires Western concepts of freedom and equality, Western achievements in industry and science. "Africa needs the West and the West needs Africa." [5] On the other hand, he tells Nkrumah "I cannot, as a man of African descent brought up in the West, recommend with good faith the agitated doctrines and promises of the hard-faced men of the West. . . . Have no illusions regarding Western attitudes. Westerners, high and low, feel that their codes, ideals, and conceptions of humanity do not apply to black men." [6] Although Wright declares his approach to be open and pragmatic, there is no gainsaying the intensity of his feelings. He is constantly "thunderstruck," "dumbfounded," "stunned," "nonplussed," "startled," and "filled with pathos" at what he sees and hears. Finally, his intellectual predilections have already been formed regarding the interpretations he is going to make. He cites throughout his work no less than nine books which have aided him in his understanding of his African experience. These sources, he assures his readers, are "exclusively bourgeois" although his analysis is to be "to a limited degree, Marxist," since Marxism strikes him as the most meaningful method of comprehending certain facts.

Some of Wright's principal concerns in *Black Power* hearken back to the themes of *Black Boy* and *12 Million Black Voices*: the psychology of the oppressed, the psychology of the oppressor, and the adjustments oppressed and oppressors must make to the changing demands of history. Generally, Wright regards the black African personality as being more or less the disordered product of a European imperialism that has shattered or weakened the integrated, orderly life of tribal society by introducing alien customs and religions. Yet here Wright, apparently in spite of himself, was most appalled by the filth, poverty, and degradation he discovered among the Ashanti whose tribal society, he tells us, was the least affected by imperialism. Utterly dominated by a fetish-type religion that teaches them to live in dread of their dead ancestors, they possess no durable ego and are unable to discern the differences between dreams and reality. Polygamy, ritual murder, and slavery are not unknown among them.

Perhaps the Africans with whom Wright most unknowingly identifies himself are the detribalized masses who live in the cities and villages of the coastal region. Cut off from their tribal environment and alienated from the Western world by race prejudice and economic discrimination, they dwell in a marginal world which provides them with no satisfactory outlet for their emotional needs. Imbued with a sense of shame for their primitive past, largely as a result of missionary efforts to convert them to Christianity, they nonetheless fall back on their primal cultural patterns of religious and emotional response at critical moments in their lives. They both resent and envy their white masters—confide in them and distrust them. For these displaced persons in their native land,

Nkrumah's cry for freedom is a substitutive religious emotion which fills the gap created in their lives by their marginal status.

Their redemption, Wright believes, lies in the sense of pride and dignity they would derive as free citizens of an independent political state. Yet, should independence be achieved, the task of making them whole men again would be enormous. Their shattered personalities, lying somewhere between a Stone Age frame of reference and twentieth century rationalism, must be forced to coalesce, to harden, so that their undertaking will succeed. For true independence in the twentieth century requires that their state be put on an industrial footing—and this, in turn, demands an immense, purposeful, dedicated marshalling of the total energies of the people. How would this come about given the psychological disarray that now exists?

Wright believes that Nkrumah must enlist and rechannel the frustrated religious energies of the detribalized masses into the holy cause of industrialism and nationhood. The extent to which Nkrumah has thus far succeeded as a political leader is the extent to which he has managed to infuse the masses with the notion that he is their new chief to whom they must direct their whole allegiance. In addition Wright calls for the total militarization of African life whereby Nkrumah would be able to use people in lieu of Western capital investment (always suspect!) to build an industrial economy. An army society would thus "atomize the fetish-ridden past, abolish the mystical and nonsensical family relations . . . [and] render impossible those parasitic chiefs." [7]

The solutions Wright suggests, one feels, are as fraught with difficulties as the problems he poses. One wonders if there would exist any real qualitative difference for the ordinary African between his thralldom to a tribal chief and thralldom to a military dictator. But even assuming he were "freer" under a totalitarian regime, there is no guarantee he would be economically better off. The machinery and the technological and managerial skills required to build a modern economy cannot be created out of a vacuum—even with the best will in the world. In all likelihood some outside help would be needed. But Wright's fear of Western neo-colonialism is almost matched by the despair and revulsion of much of what he has seen in Africa. (Wright was even more discouraged about Africa than he admitted in his book. He wrote his agent Paul Reynolds in New York, "you asked for something on the uplift in the African book, but I'm afraid that it cannot be. I was afraid at what I found here; and yet I'm told that the Gold Coast is by far the best part of Africa. If that is so, I don't want to see the worst.")

Wright reserves his bitterest scorn for the black bourgeoisie and minor government officials who do not share Nkrumah's hopes for immediate independence. To a remarkable degree they resemble the Negro middle classes whom Wright so detested in the United States. They identify themselves with their British masters (the clerks in business establishments even wear heavy woolens in Accra's intolerable heat) and have adopted similar political and social views. Many of them feel that Africa's black masses are not prepared for independence, a view that Wright, in spite of himself, shared to a certain extent, and regard Nkrumah's demands for radical constitutional changes as dangerous and preposterous. They obviously fear for their hard-won struggle for status, should real independence be achieved.

Although Wright opposes Nkrumah's intellectual opponents, he finds them more appealing than the black bourgeoisie. By and large he discovers them smarting from a sense of betrayal ever since the British had "generously" undertaken to recognize Nkrumah's political legitimacy. (He had, a year before, been released from jail.) A number of them had attained renown in Western academic circles (Doctors Ampofo, Busia, and Danquah), and to Wright's dismay they all talk more openly and frankly to him than do the reserved and suspicious leaders of the Convention People's Party whose causes Wright supports. Although there are nationalists among them, Wright makes clear the reasons he finds their nationalism less attractive than that of Nkrumah's Convention People's Party. According to Wright, they desire that the British transfer power into the hands of a few intellectuals, chiefs, and bourgeoisie who would rule in much the same undemocratic fashion as the British. The masses would thus discover that they had only exchanged one set of masters for another. No attempt would be made at industrialization—Wright, incidentally, at one point wonders how industrialization can ever be achieved in a climate that rusts razor blades overnight—nor would they attempt to destroy the tribal structure that is responsible for Africa's stagnation. Wright's reasons for supporting the Convention People's Party, on the other hand, are that Nkrumah's mass appeal has been successfully undermining the authority of the chiefs, thereby hastening the process of detribalization—a process which was begun by the British, whom Wright condemns.

If Wright unconsciously identifies himself with Africa's detribalized natives, he explicitly identifies himself with their leaders. Or perhaps it would be more accurate to say he identifies men like Nkrumah and his aides with himself—for Wright had very little opportunity to gauge the personalities of the leaders of the CPP whom he met on his African trip. And, he complains, those that he did meet were overly reticent when they spoke about their aims or plans for the future. Yet Wright reconstructs their psychology partially out of what he knows about them, partially out of what he observes when he is with them, and partially out of his own experiences. They are, according to Wright, true Outsiders. Educated by missionaries, they are imbued with a sense of shame for their tribal past, and wish passionately to identify themselves with their new mentors. But the missionaries, for a variety of neurotic and racial reasons, are unable to practice the Christian love they preach and their novices discover themselves in a peculiar halfway world, hovering somewhere between the West that has rejected them and the tribal life which they themselves have come to reject. They begin now to hate the missionaries who have brought them to this impasse, yet they are emotionally incapable of returning to the life they had once known. (Thus far, they are not unlike any of the other detribalized masses whose culture has been smashed by the Europeans.) But, if these nascent leaders are fortunate, they travel abroad to Europe or to America where they attend universities and learn further the ways of the West. At first they are delighted by the splendid industrial and scientific achievements they discover and desire once again to identify themselves with Western values. But soon they find out that their race or their colonial status renders them second class citizens in the Western scheme of things. If they are weak and play the colonial game, they may be rewarded with lordships or minor government posts as black officials under foreign domination, but if they insist on the freedom and material advantages they have seen in the West for their own people, they are shunted aside, arrested, or persecuted. They return home dismayed but determined upon a course of action that will either bring them disgrace or national honor of the highest sort. Thus Wright's vision of the nationalist revolutionary endowed with a new sense of life as a result of his contact with the West is not unlike the sequestered Mississippi Black Boy who first hungered for personal freedom after reading forbidden books. Strange bedfellows—but who is to say that Wright's projection of his own life onto that of Africa's new leaders may not be valid?

Although it was not Wright's intention to deal with British colonials when he went to Africa, he found himself more dependent upon them than he had supposed. It was a British missionary who interpreted for him when Wright interviewed a native about his religion. It was a British police officer to whom Wright addressed his questions regarding crime in Accra. It was a British government official who told him about the linguistic problems attendant upon political unification. And it was the British Gold Coast Information Service, and not Nkrumah's government that finally planned his motor trip into Ashanti country and arranged for his sleeping accommodations at the homes of white settlers along the way. Ironically, he found them the most hospitable of any of the people he met in Africa. They assumed he shared their views regarding British policies in Africa. On one occasion he was invited to a cocktail party at which the guests vied with one another in telling derogatory jokes about the natives. Wright was expected to join in the laughter. Evidently they imagined him to be not unlike the black bourgeoisie who helped them administer their colony. A fatal error—for Wright's indictment of the British is devastating. His main conclusions about the British stem more from his sense of outrage as he observes a shattered native African civilization than from the mainly pleasant contacts he has made with the British themselves in the course of his journey.

Wright is of course at his best when he is relating something he has just seen, or recording one of his own conversations. The portraits he paints of black Africans are better supported by the experiences he has had among them than the generalizations he makes about white men which are supported by little evidence at all. Yet his eye is good and his instincts are sound, and if he is sometimes unfair to those Englishmen who care as genuinely for the welfare of Africa as Wright himself, he probably captures the essential character of the majority of white colonials when he writes of them that their situation breeds in them a kind of indifference, a "hopeless laziness" and an "easy going contempt for human life existing in a guise [so] strange and offensive." [8] Regardless of how they attempt to delude themselves, they are uneasy with natives because, at bottom, they know they are stealing from them. Africa for most Europeans, Wright continues, is a "dingy mirror" on which they project their own personalities, their own base motives and desires. Africa today is despoiled and torn because "the rejected and self-despised of Europe" have attempted to destroy in Africa what they most loathe and hate in themselves.

There is something about this book suggestive of both a travel diary and of a writer's journal of ideas as well. Yet whenever Wright feels that a point he is making may be better illustrated by information he has gleaned outside of personal observations, he does not hesitate to use such material at appropriate times. There are, for example, statistical charts indicating marriage dowries and fines for adultery which he has obtained from tribal sources. Nor does he fail to mention relevant historical data that he has gathered from the books he carries about with him. Wright is however, at his best when he employs his novelist's techniques. Much of his account is interlaced with dialogue as Wright questions tribal chieftains, British officials, politicians, intellectuals and business men — and often their answers are as revealing as anything Wright could point to in expository language. In addition, Wright suggests mood or intensity of feeling by invoking movement or change in the external environment. (He does this in his fiction as well because so many of his protagonists are inarticulate.) Wright often applies this method (a kind of prose "objective correlative") to express his reactions or point of view. For example, after attending a cocktail party at which the guests had been amusing themselves by ridiculing the natives, Wright returns to his bungalow and prepares for bed.

> Jungle lay out there. Then I started, my skin prickling. A sound came to my ears out of the jungle night; something — it was a tree bear, I was told afterwards — began a dreadful kind of moaning that stabbed the heart. It began like a baby crying, then it ascended to

a sort of haunting scream, followed by a weird kind of hooting that was essence of despair. The sound kept on and on, sobbing, seemingly out of breath, as if the heart was so choked with sorrow that another breath could not be drawn. Finally, a moan came at long intervals, as though issuing from a body in the last extremities of physical suffering. And when I could no longer hear it, I still felt that it was sounding in my mind.[9]

It would not be until another four years after Wright had left Africa that Ghana achieved her independence. The birth pangs of independence which Wright had attempted to describe have been attended with success but subsequent events have proved that the enormous problems—political, economic, and psychological—which Wright pointed to, remain and will undoubtedly take generations before they can begin to be resolved. Perhaps Wright's principal achievement was his imaginative grasp of the human and historical implications of the emergence of Africa. The transformation of a Stone Age people into a modern nation is indeed one of the most stunning events of history—whose real significance few Western writers have even yet come to realize. To an amazing degree one feels Wright has understood the psychology of the new African with far greater depth than the seeming casualness and informality of his style would imply. If Wright appears at times too harsh, too contradictory, too suspicious, it would be well to remember that in a sense Wright reflects the attitudes of the African leaders with whom he was so much in sympathy. Justified or not, this is the reality that the West must face. For years Wright had been carrying on a love-hate affair with the West. Perhaps his angry rejection of the West was the sincerest expression of his love.

In *Pagan Spain* Wright continued his pursuit of the identity of oppressed people. But the new militancy and vigor Wright thought he had detected among the

rising generation of Negro youth whom he had stud-
ied some fourteen years earlier in 12 *Million Black
Voices* were nowhere to be found among the Spaniards he observed in 1954. Instead he discovered them
to be floundering in an idealized past whose rituals and
psychology Wright could only regard as primitive or
pagan. Such a pagan view of life he described as being
"a love of ritual and ceremony; a delight in color and
movement and sound . . . an extolling of sheer emotion . . . a deification of tradition . . . a continuous
lisping about greatness, honor, glory, bravery" and a
sense of overlordship to the morally and spiritually
inferior.[10] Indeed so pessimistic was Wright's appraisal
of Spanish civilization that he thought that the rising
nations of Africa—for all their problems of tribalism
and technological backwardness—had a far better
chance of surviving the trials and difficulties of the
twentieth century. Wright went to Spain with the
usual intellectual and emotional predispositions of the
humanitarian liberal left. He had a lingering nostalgia
for the lost Loyalist cause he had supported during the
Spanish Civil War; he had a hatred of clericalism and
an intense distrust of all forms of religious belief; he
was opposed on principle and out of personal experience to the police state and all kinds of oppressive
authoritative rule, and he possessed a pragmatic socialist vision of what constitutes the good society. None
of these views was shaken, and possibly a number of
them were confirmed by his visit to Spain, but he
came, in time, to regard them as irrelevant for understanding the Spanish psychology. In a sense the conclusions Wright drew were arrived at on the spot as a
result of the interviews he had with Spaniards of various classes, of experiences he underwent as he trav-
elled through the country, and of observations he
made as he sat in bull rings, watched religious festivals
and contemplated the Spanish landscape. Insofar as
Wright applied any a priori concepts in his approach,
they were Freudian, but not in any intrusive or patronizing sense.

Superficially, the book appears to be a rambling, discursive, impressionistic account of a motor trip Wright took through Spain in the late summer of 1954, and again in the first few months of 1955. But a second glance reveals that *Pagan Spain* has a closer unity than Wright's casual manner would seem to indicate. First, there is the unity of purpose: Wright aims to penetrate the heart of the Spanish experience; every event he records, every interview he reports, every observation he makes is directed toward highlighting some aspect of the Spanish psychology—so that as the book draws to a close it is possible for Wright to make certain inductions from what at first appear to be random notes and impressions of his journey. Secondly, there is a unity of structure. The book is divided into five chapters, the first four of which illustrate variations on a theme announced in each of the chapter headings. Thus, the first chapter, "Life After Death," refers to the day-to-day existence and the political, social, and economic attitudes of the average Spaniard after the death of the Republic. There is ironic allusion as well, of course, to the eschatological promises of Christianity and the Church which Wright felt were depriving the people of their mortal and material happiness. The second chapter, "Death and Exaltation," deals with Wright's discovery that a morbid prepossession with violence, death and sex, otherwise repressed, are celebrated and objectified in the two principal institutions of Spanish culture—the bull ring and the Church. The next chapter, "The Underground Christ," records a lengthy interview Wright had with one of Spain's twenty thousand Protestants. The subtle and overt methods by which the State persecuted and terrorized non-Catholics convinced Wright that Spanish Protestants were Spain's Negroes—and that the Spanish Protestant's psyche was similar to that of the southern American Negro. The theme of the fourth chapter, "Sex, Flamenco, and Prostitution," relates Wright's firsthand observations regarding the connection between poverty and prostitution, and concludes that the Spanish cult of the Virgin and the Church's attitude toward sin account for sex being the major preoccupation of Spaniards, and prostitution being Spain's major industry. "The World of Pagan Power," Wright's final chapter, is, in effect, a summary and amplification of his previously announced themes, from which he draws the inevitable conclusion that Spain is gripped in the vice of a pre-rational, pre-Christian frame of mind and that the Spanish Catholic Church is the principal instrument through which this is expressed.

Although Wright makes scarcely any direct allusion to the role of the State in condemning the Spanish people to a pagan way of life, he does reproduce verbatim in each of his chapters questions and answers from a required political text for Spanish girls (aged nine to seventeen) which underscore his main argument and illumine the different ways in which the Falangist political philosophy reflects the total pagan atmosphere. Thus, in his chapter "Death and Exaltation," after having defined the "spiritual exercise" of the bullfighter as being "the conquering of fear, the making of a religion of the conquering of fear," Wright picks up his political text and reads about José Antonio, the founder of the Falangist Party who in effect is expected to exercise the same spiritual energies as the bullfighter. For it is courage, the conquest of fear—not social intelligence—that is the most highly prized attribute of the politician. Sometimes the Falangist political catechism serves as an ironic commentary on the professed ideals of the civilization. On one occasion Wright describes how an American woman traveling alone is humiliated and insulted by the landlord of her pension, who regards her as a whore because she is unchaperoned. After Wright rescues her, he turns to his political catechism and reads that women's heroism "consists more in doing well what they have to do every day than in dying heroically." [11]

One of Wright's principal strengths as an author of

fiction lay in his ability to convey in vivid visual terms
violence, suspense, movement, and action. And in
Pagan Spain Wright draws on these skills to elicit the
color, brilliance, and excitement of the bull ring. His
accounts of bull fights are small masterpieces of torea-
dor literature and vie with the best that has been
written in English. Here, for example, Wright, in a
mounting crescendo of phrases builds up the charging
excitement of the bull's physical presence:

> That startling black hair, that madly slashing tail, that
> bunched and flexed mountain of neck and shoulder
> muscles, that almost hog-like distension of the wet and
> inflated and dripping nostrils, that defiant and careless
> lack of control of the anal passage, that continuous
> throbbing of the thin, trembling flanks, that open-
> mouthed panting that was so rapid that it resembled a
> prolonged shivering, that ever ready eagerness to attack
> again and again that was evidenced by those fluid shift-
> ings of his massive and mobile weight from hoof to
> hoof.[12]

But sometimes, in order to lend credence to his insights, Wright reaches for images that are so blatantly
obvious that they damage his claim to objectivity. The
essence of the Church's appeal in Spain, he says, lies
in its mythic sexual symbolism. In relating an ascent
to Montserrat to visit the shrine of the Black Virgin,
he describes the cluster of rock along the roadway as
"nations of seriated phalluses, each rocky republic of
erections rising higher than its predecessor." [13]

As in *Black Boy*, Wright employs dialogue to engage the reader in the immediacy of any situation in
which he is involved. But now Wright's confrontations are not exclusively designed to arouse the reader's feelings of outrage and anger. Rather do they
present his intellectual difficulties as well, as he tries to
understand his environment. Part of the charm of
Pagan Spain is that Wright introduces the reader into
his thought processes as he attempts to solve them.
("There was something missing here. There was not

enough psychological food in this home to sustain a genuinely human life. What was there that linked this family with the modern world? . . . Ah, I had it. They had the Church!") [14]

Although Wright regarded Spain as being hopelessly mired in an archaic past, he was much too compassionate to raise his voice in anger. (Once when Wright was asked whether he liked Spain, he answered diplomatically, "I like the people.") There is nothing of the polemical, the strident, or the patronizing in Wright's tone. When he speaks of Spanish women, there is an untypical note of warmth and sympathy in his voice. "Stalwart, they bear the burdens of their poor nation and with but few complaints . . . [they knit] together in a web of care and love what would otherwise be a senseless anarchy." [15] Even when Wright discusses the Church, the principal villain of the piece, he is moved to understand it in historical terms. Spain, he writes, was not even in the modern Western sense Christian. The pagan strains of Goths, Greeks, Jews, Romans, Iberians, and Moors were much too powerful for Western Christianity to dispel. And the early victory in Spain of Catholicism, "itself burdened with a paganism that it had sought vainly to digest, had here in Spain been sucked into the maw of a paganism buried deep in the hearts of the people." [16] In the final analysis Wright's diagnosis of the sickness of Spanish civilization rests on theoretical grounds. As might be expected the book was roundly denounced in Catholic circles, but for others, such as Herbert Matthews, the New York Times reporter, who had lived through the Civil War, Wright had remarkable insights into the Spanish character. In certain respects, however, a proper evaluation of the book depends to some extent on an understanding of the man who wrote it. One suspects that Wright, in going to Spain, was in a sense seeking his own past. Perhaps he felt that his European experience provided him with a greater degree of objectivity than he had ever hitherto known—and that by investigating the roots of oppression, he would be better able to reassess the experiences of his youth. (Once, years before, he had insisted to John Steinbeck in Mexico that he intended to return to New York via the Jim Crow country of the deep South so that his memories wouldn't grow dim.) In any event, he posited his Outsider's sense of freedom as a point of reference from which he would study the nature of the Spanish people. "I have no religion in the formal sense of the word. . . . I have no race except that which is forced upon me. I have no country except that to which I am obliged to belong. I have no traditions. I'm free. I have only the future." [17]

Wright regarded his Outsider freedom as being part of his Western Protestant heritage and contrasted it to the psychological imprisonment of Spanish Catholicism. The Spaniard's image of a better world depends upon a display of external symbols: the rites, rituals, adornments, and pageantry of the Church that have forced his imagination and frozen his emotions—but Protestants, for whom these trappings are an anathema, have projected their longings onto their natural environment and have thus created their "sense of God out of the worldliness of the world," their civilization out of the materials they have found in the natural world. The social systems of Protestant countries therefore "had higher standards of living, more health, more literacy, more industry—all stemming from the Protestant's ability to handle the materials of reality."

It may well be that Wright's view of the role of the Church in Spain is a projection in historical terms of the oppressive role his Seventh Day Adventist upbringing played on his own development. ("I was born a Protestant. I lived a Protestant childhood. But I feel more or less toward that religion as Protestants in Spain feel toward Catholicism.") [18] Moreover, Wright himself had to conjure up out of *his* imagination a

4

The Shattered Civilization
The Color Curtain; White Man, Listen!

Some time in December of 1954, Wright returned to
Paris from Spain in order to join his family for Christ-
mas. He remembers picking up a newspaper one day
in his Paris apartment and reading about a proposed
summit meeting of twenty-nine Afro-Asian nations
scheduled for the following spring in Indonesia. The
prospect of the Bandung Conference thrilled him:

> My God! I began a rapid calculation of the popu-
> lations of the nations listed and, when my total topped
> the billion mark, I stopped. . . . The despised, the in-
> sulted, the hurt, the dispossessed—in short, the under-
> dogs of the human race were meeting . . . it smacked
> of tidal waves, of natural forces.[1]

Wright, at the recommendation of his friend, Gunnar
Myrdal, got in touch with the editors of *Preuves*, and
arranged through them to be sent to Indonesia as a
press representative for the Congress of Cultural Freedom. Wright was convinced that the proposed
Conference went beyond mere ideology. "The agenda,
and subject matter," he asserted, "had been written
for centuries in the blood and bones of the participants. The conditions under which these men had
lived had become their tradition, their culture, their
raison d'être." [2] Wright felt that his own experiences
as a Western "colonial" who in the past knew "something of the politics and psychology of rebellion" ad-
mirably prepared him for his task. He next got in

touch with Otto Klineberg, the American psychologist, who had done a number of studies on the psychological disabilities of American Negroes. Klineberg helped Wright arrange a series of questions which he intended to put to Africans and Asians whom he met abroad. The questions themselves were all oriented toward discovering character conflict in persons who might presumably have mixed feelings about their color. (As it happened, Wright later found he had no use for his questionnaire in Indonesia. The Asians and Africans whom he met in Jakarta and Bandung were uninhibited in expressing their racial feelings, particularly when they felt there were no whites around. But Wright did ask his questions of Asians whom he met in Europe and their answers are recorded in his book.) Wright returned to Spain sometime later in January of 1955 to gather more material for his book on Spain. On April 10, 1955, he boarded a plane at Madrid for the first lap of his journey to Asia. The meaning of that journey he recorded in *The Color Curtain* (1955).

Wright's thesis in *The Color Curtain* is that "race" is the central issue that determines the mood, the vagaries, and possibly the political and ideological directions of the new nations of Africa and Asia. Since the West has for centuries rationalized its rule over Asia and Africa in terms of race superiority (explicitly or implicitly), the "colored" nations of the world are understandably sensitive and suspicious of the West and Western motives. Hence, despite vast differences in culture, religion, and traditions, the issue of race has bound the peoples of Asia and Africa together as no other issue could. As in *Black Power*, Wright re-avers the theme that the introduction of alien strains of Western culture has all but debilitated once-flourishing civilizations, and that the nations of Africa and Asia must set for themselves new goals in order to regenerate psychological and political health.

In a real sense, Wright felt, this was the reason the

Conference was called. The new nations were now facing an uncertain future with no past history to guide them. The Conference was intended to establish and explore political, cultural, and economic ties in order to make the common travail of the new nations less agonizing. The legacy of colonialism—economic exploitation and racism—had sapped their strength and rendered them vulnerable to all sorts of internal disorders and external threats of Communism and neo-imperialism. Wherever Wright went, he heard the new leaders affirming industrialism as the principal means by which their nations might restore themselves to a sense of dignity. For one thing it would get the West "off their backs" and end what they regarded as their nations' intolerable economic dependence. Secondly, despite their rejection of Western racism and materialism, they saw European technology as a gauge by which they could measure their countries' modernity and maturity. It was for them undeniably a matter of racial and national pride that the new nations prove themselves capable of handling the tools and technology of the West. Wright, himself, believed that Western science and industry could provide the colored masses with an alternative rational basis of life as opposed to the violent, irrational emotionalism of race and religion that had been sweeping through vast areas of the colored world.

In *The Color Curtain* Wright's views regarding the problems of the Afro-Asian nations are not notably at variance with the ones he had expressed two years earlier in his African study, *Black Power*. One difference, however, lies in his treatment of the West's relationship to the underdeveloped areas of the world. It will be recalled that in *Black Power*, Wright had cautioned Nkrumah against accepting any assistance from the West on the grounds that such help might invite new forms of imperialism and exploitation. But in Asia, Wright was even more appalled at the poverty, the industrial backwardness, and the volcanic racial feelings of the Afro-Asian colored masses and thus concluded that only an immediate and massive program of Western capital and technological assistance could save the situation from deteriorating further. Such a program, Wright believed, must inevitably lower the standard of living of the West since its cost would be enormous. In addition, those areas of the world which now serve as markets and raw producers for Western industry would eventually become self-sufficient, thereby reducing Western profit and investment opportunities. Yet the alternative for the West, in Wright's view, would be an explosive racial war or a brutal, bloody Stalinization of the new countries in order that they might meet the exacting, competitive standards of a Western economy.

As in *Black Power*, Wright is remarkably impressed by the "Westernized leaders of the new countries who must employ demagogic means to organize their nations on a rational basis." In effect, he declares, like their Stalinist counterparts in Russia and China, they apply the sorely inadequate materials they find at hand in order to refashion their states along modern lines. And what are the materials? They are the antiquated and atrophied social institutions—a legacy of their colonial past—and the explosive racial and religious energies that have been released as a by-product of independence. Nkrumah, like Lenin, Wright points out, had already successfully organized his "partly truncated tribal" nation into a modern state, and Sukarno, like Mao-Tse-tung, is not above appealing to racial feelings. "Sukarno was appealing to race and religion; they were the only realities in the lives of the men before him that he could appeal to. . . . Sukarno was not evoking these twin demons; he was not trying to create them; he was trying to organize them." [3]

Although one need not quarrel with the view that many of the Afro-Asian nations require drastic rehabilitation, it does not seem to occur to Wright that possibly their new leaders may use race simply to

maintain themselves in power. But practically all of
Wright's political views are derived ultimately from
his observations of the characterological effects of racism among those who have been directly or indirectly
involved in the colored areas of the world. In *The
Color Curtain*, Wright's investigations go beyond the
several groups who compose the various segments of
colonial society. Wright asks questions of Europeans
who seldom think of Asia except as an appendage of
Europe. He deals with white "liberal" Americans, and
conscience-ridden Dutch businessmen who remain on
in Indonesia in an exploitative capacity. He notes the
attendance of American Negroes at Bandung and tries
to account for their presence in psychological terms.
He speaks of persons of mixed European and Asian
blood who are unable to identify with either community. He gathers insights from the faces of the ordinary
Jakarta citizens as they watch the procession of foreign
dignitaries move in and out of their city. And finally,
he reserves his greatest sympathy for the colored,
Western-educated intellectuals and leaders of the new
nations who are outsiders to their own cultures. For
each, the problems of racial identity has created terrible moral and psychic scars. It is Wright's contention
that the idealistic resolutions passed at the Conference
calling for economic, and political cooperation, cultural liaison, and political autonomy for the remaining
colonies are, in the final analysis, derived from the
racial inequities the colored masses of the world have
suffered over the centuries. The leaders at the Conference, Wright stresses, are Westernized in the sense
that their premises and actions are based on rational,
secular considerations. Should these leaders be displaced by Stalinists or racial or religious extremists,
Western civilization itself would be endangered. The
Conference then was addressed as much to the West
as it was to the peoples of Asia and Africa; it was a
solemn warning to the West that a milestone in world
affairs had been reached. For the first time the colored

peoples of the world had found their voice and had been able to express their agonies and their dreams in no uncertain terms.

When sometime later in Paris Wright was told that John Foster Dulles had described the Conference as a "little fish fry," Wright snorted, "THEM FISH WAS WHALES, BROTHER!" [4] There can, however, be little doubt that Wright in some ways overestimated the significance of the Conference. The much publicized "solidarity" was more apparent than real, and subsequent years have proved the existence of centrifugal forces of national aspirations and cultural and ethnic differences. Had Wright been a less enthusiastic observer, he might have been better able to see these divisions shaping up in Bandung. Latter day conferences of neutralist or non-aligned countries have been less representative of the political realities that obtain within the colored world. This has been particularly true in Africa where several groupings of nations have coalesced in regional or ideological blocs and barred other nations of the continent from participating in their plans. Wright was, however, correct in gauging the depth of racial intensity among these "colored" nations—witness the unanimity of their votes in the United Nations whenever issues of apartheid, human rights, or colonialism arise.

Prime Minister Nehru of India was the leader whom Wright admired most at Bandung. He was a pragmatic Marxist (as opposed to the dogmatic variety of the Communists) oriented toward Western ideals of freedom and rationalism. It may have been for this reason that Wright was somewhat misled as to the wisdom, propriety, or *realpolitik* of Nehru's invitation to Chou En-lai to attend the Conference. Wright's view was that Nehru felt that Afro-Asian unity required Communist China's attendance despite the risk of China's aggressive intentions. According to Wright a united front with China must have seemed to Nehru to represent a less significant danger than the predatory potentialities of the West. There could be no real unity in Asia without China. And a "multi-nationed agreement with China, would perhaps give the other non-Communist nations a chance of standing against China if she were caught cheating." [5] Yet if Wright's understanding of Nehru's motives is correct, it does not appear, in the light of India's 1962 border war with China, that the support Nehru hoped he would get from the Afro-Asian powers has been realized. Indeed, China's attendance at the Conference may have mitigated some of the fervent anti-China sentiments among some of the delegates. (One pro-Western delegate, according to Wright, was so impressed by Chou En-lai that he remarked afterwards, "I'm as violently opposed to Communism as ever. But I trust this man.") [6]

But even granting certain miscalculations on Nehru's part, it is questionable whether China's presence at the Conference did any irreparable damage to the Afro-Asian cause. Allowing for the most sinister aims of the Communist Chinese, it is difficult to see what the Afro-Asians might have gained by keeping the Chinese out. As regards China's real purposes at Bandung, Wright could only conjecture. He observed a possible divergence of tactics between Russia and China and suggested that wider differences might be in the offing. He noted that the Chinese carefully refrained from defending the attacks that were being made on Russian foreign policy in the closed committees. He conjectured too, judging from the passive, all but accommodating attitude of the Communist Chinese, that they might not be averse to playing on sensitive racial issues in order to extend their influence. That such a policy would alienate Russia is, of course, obvious. It is some measure of Wright's political acumen that he did not in 1955 envision the Communist "monolith" (Russia and China) as being eternally cohesive—a more sophisticated view than some Western nations entertained at that time.

Superficially, *The Color Curtain* gives the impression of being a well written piece of popular journalism. Wright adopts an informal, almost casual tone in relating his impressions and interpretations of events at Bandung. On occasion he resorts to personal anecdotes or describes incidents about which he has been told secondhand. Yet there is an undertone of deep seriousness to the whole piece whose appeal lies below the surface of events. It is here, one senses, Wright the artist speaks:

> I felt while at Bandung that the English language was about to undergo one of the most severe tests in its long and glorious history. . . . Alien pressures and structures of thought and feeling will be brought to bear upon this our mother tongue and we shall be hearing some strange and twisted expression. . . . But this is all to the good; a language is useless unless it can be used for the vital purposes of life, and to use a language in new situations is, inevitably, to change it.
>
> Thus, the strident moral strictures against the Western world preached at Bandung were uttered in the language of the cultures that the delegates were denouncing! I felt that there was something just and proper about it; by this means English was coming to contain a new extension of feeling, of moral knowledge.[7]

For Wright then the chief significance of Bandung lay in its poetic meaning. It was the triumphant but agonized cry of freedom of a billion and a half of the world's people. It was a cry for help mingled with a proud defiance of those from whom help was being asked. Would the West hear and understand? Should the West fail the East, the very foundations of civilization would be endangered—the civilization of which Wright felt so very much a part.

White Man, Listen! is a collection of four lectures Wright delivered in Europe between 1950 and 1956. Three of the four deal with the West's relationship to emerging nations of Asia and Africa—and the remaining one, with the Negro writer's place in American letters. As the title suggests, the core of these lectures represents a solemn warning to the West that the colored masses of the world no longer intend to stand passively by and allow the white nations of the West to determine their place in world affairs. In essence, they describe the baleful effects of racism, and the problems racism has created for the modern world. The views Wright expresses here are, in effect, identical to the ones he has stated in the works already discussed. Indeed they appear to be the intellectual framework out of which his works of nonfiction have been fashioned. Hence there is no necessity to discuss Wright's ideas in this work. It might, however, be instructive to recount in skeleton form Wright's intellectual position from the order in which he presents his material, since the lectures Wright offers his readers in this book are not given in the same chronology as he delivered them. One may assume therefore that Wright, in constructing the book, intended to develop a certain sequential logic.

Wright dedicated his book to the "tragic elite," the new leaders of Asia and Africa and the West Indies, who like himself, are sufficiently outside the subjective, irrational passions of East and West to want to build their nations on the best principles of "both worlds." The outsider theme informs each of the pieces for apparently it is only "the lonely outsiders" dwelling on the "margins of many cultures" who are the free men capable of establishing free societies. Freedom, then, is the central issue around which all his essays revolve. Wright follows the dedication with two poetic fragments posing the conflict between psychological bondage and emotional freedom. The first of these is from Blake's "London."

> *In every cry of every Man,*
> *In every Infant's cry of fear,*
> *In every voice, in every ban,*
> *The mind-forg'd manacles I hear.*

The response is from Dylan Thomas's "Light Breaks Where No Sun Shines." Even in the unlikeliest recesses of the heart, freedom lurks; the spirit yearns to be free. Part of the fragment Wright reproduces reads as follows:

> *Light breaks on secret lots,*
> *On tips of thoughts where thoughts smell in the rain;*
> *When logics die,*
> *The secret of the soil grows through the eye,*
> *And blood jumps in the sun . . .*

Hence freedom like a biological instinct is the psychological imperative. It is the quality of the human heart out of which societies are born and civilization built.

In his "Author's Introduction" Wright affirms that he is a free-man—made free, made an outsider, by his marginal status as an American Negro. Hence, if what he is about to say is not comforting, it is at least true. "I do not deal in happiness; I deal in meaning."

If the basis for freedom is psychological, so is the basis for slavery. In his first piece, "The Psychological Reactions of Oppressed Peoples," Wright is concerned with showing the underlying emotions of subject peoples. As we have seen in *Black Power*, the conquerors are driven as much by their passions as by the material advantages they may gain—but Wright is, of course, most interested in describing the effects of oppression on the conquered—from blind adoration to self-hating obsequiousness. The body of the lecture is given over to a cataloging of a variety of reactions. The free men are those natives among the conquered who have learned too well the rational and secular principles on which Western civilization is based (the "tragic elite" outsiders again) and attempt to relate these to the building of their own countries.

From the psychological freedom of the human heart to the practical projection of this freedom onto external reality is the theme of Wright's second piece, "Tradition and Industrialization." Here Wright views

the rational principles of Western industry and science as the best means of weaning the colored masses
away from the psychological bondage of their tribal
customs and religions. The next step in the process
toward total freedom is described in "The Literature
of the Negro in the United States." In this piece (a
modified version of a lecture Wright had from time to
time delivered in the United States in 1945) Wright
presents a cursory survey of Negro letters from colonial times to the present. Wright believes that the
Negro's assimilation as a Westerner toward total freedom and equality may be traced through his literature.
Insofar as his letters are concerned totally or predomi-
nantly with racial themes, the Negro is still regarded
—and regards himself often enough—as a subspecies of
the human race. Where race themes do not predomi-
nate in his literature, then the reader may assume that
progress is being made toward equality. Wright finds
encouraging signs in the works of young Negro writers
in this regard. His final piece, "The Miracle of Nationalism in the African Gold Coast," describes in part the
workings of the rare free men, the "outsiders" of Africa, in winning independence for the Gold Coast.
Although the means they have pursued in achieving
their goals may appear to the West subtle and devious, the West must support these men as the only
alternative to explosive racism in Africa.

Hence the lectures describe a pattern of progress
from emotional and political bondage to freedom.
The significance and implications of Wright's ideas
have been discussed elsewhere, but it would be well
here to observe again a few of the basic elements in
Wright's thinking. The achievement of freedom is an
individual and private affair, a struggle that is won in
the hearts of some men regardless of the external and
environmental circumstances in which they find themselves. Their freedom is their rationality, but they discover themselves outsiders—a tragic elite, like
Nietzche's Zarathustra—to the myth-bound passions

of self-awareness—an immediate knowledge that the world in which the protagonist dwells is chaotic, meaningless, purposeless, and that he, as a Negro, is "outside" this world and must therefore discover his own life by his lonely individual thoughts and acts. We find thus in these first short stories a kind of black nationalism wedded to what has been called Wright's existentialism—the principal characteristics of Wright's last phase of political and philosophical thinking.

Paradoxically, Wright's Marxism seldom intrudes in an explicit didactic sense (although it was to do so on occasion in his later works, even after he left the Party). Perhaps this was because he had so ingested the concepts of struggle and conflict as being the central facts of life that he had little need to remind himself that the strife he was describing was ideological. Although Marxist dialectic must have provided Wright with a clear-cut arena on which he could observe the struggle of the oppressed and the oppressors, the reader is left with the nagging feeling that this was not quite the same way in which the Communists saw the class struggle in the 1930's. (In this connection it is interesting to note that some years later Wright admitted some Communist officials asked him if he really wrote the book.) To be sure, Communists are viewed in a kindly light in the last two of Wright's stories, but they are only remotely instrumental in effecting his heroes' discovery of themselves and their world. Oddly enough, in three of the stories ("Down by the Riverside," "Fire and Cloud," and "Bright and Morning Star"), Wright's simple Negro peasants arrive at their sense of self-realization by applying basic Christian principles to the situations in which they find themselves. In only one ("Bright and Morning Star"), does a character convert to Communism—and then only when she discovers Communism is the modern translation of the primitive Christian values she has always lived. There is a constant identification in these stories with the fleeing Hebrew children of the Old Testament and the persecuted Christ—and mood, atmosphere, and settings abound in Biblical nuances. Wright's characters die like martyrs, stoic and unyielding, in their new-found truth about themselves and their vision of a freer, fuller world for their posterity. Sarah, of "Long Black Song," lost in her dreams of love and simple understanding among men, stands as the primitive prototype of the madonna as she suckles her infant at her breast. The spare, stark accounts of actions and their resolution are reminiscent in their simplicity and their cadences of Biblical narrations. The floods, the songs, the sermons, the hymns reinforce the Biblical analogies and serve, ironically, to highlight the uselessness and inadequacy of Christianity as a means of coping with the depression-ridden, racist South. Even the reverse imagery of white-evil, black-good is suggestive in its simple organization of the forces which divide the world in Old Testament accounts of the Hebrews' struggle for survival.

In *Uncle Tom's Children,* unlike most modern short stories, the complexities of the narrative line, the twists and turns of the plot, are essential for an understanding of the characters' feelings and the nuances of their emotions. As opposed to the stories of Chekhov or Joyce, say, a good deal "happens" in Wright's short stories. The reasons are clear when one considers the kind of characters Wright is dealing with. They are, for the most part, uneducated, inarticulate, and have had neither the time nor inclination to cultivate or verbalize their feelings in their terrible struggle for physical survival. Hence Wright must show them for what they are in terms of their reactions to certain situations—particularly in situations where violence and rank injustices cry out for immediate decisions. They are sometimes in flight after having killed a white person—and their recognition of their hatred is their first sense of freedom. Often Wright describes their mood in terms of a raging landscape or sunlit

fields or the desolate sky which feeds upon their senses
and draws out their hearts in the actions they perform.
But more often he is successful in delineating their
character by means of the dialogue they employ. Since
their vocabularies are limited, they are compelled to
convey meaning in terms of gesture, tone, and voice
volume. Folk idiom and rhythms are maintained as
much as possible (spelling is often phonetic) and conversations are rendered in dialect. To indicate shouts,
significant voice emphases, or jarring revelations,
Wright frequently spells out his words in upper case
letters. (A Negro who has been forcibly separated
from his dying wife in order to work on the flood-
threatened levee shouts out his anguish, "AHM TIRED!
LEMME GO WID MAH FOLKS, PLEASE!") Sounds of violence which are so much a part of their lives and
consciousness are recreated onomatopoetically. Rifles
"CRACK!," whips "whick," white terrorists creep up
on their prey in the wet grass "cush-cush," exploding
steam is rendered "Psseeeezzzzzzzzzzzzzzzzzzzz . . ."
Again Wright suggests the kind of characters they are
by songs they sing. The raucous, bawdy adolescents of
"Big Boy Leaves Home," sing snatches from the
Negro "Dirty Dozens." Sarah, the mother earth figure
of "Long Black Song" croons lullabies to her sleeping
child and makes love to the surging rhythms of a
gospel song. Sue, the mother of two adult sons, in
"Bright and Morning Star" is converted to Communism because the Communist vision of a better life
satisfies her deeply imbued religious nature, represented by a hymn which she sings over and over again
half to herself throughout the story.

Although Wright's characters move toward a kind
of inevitable doom because they have violated the
impossible conditions of their caste, their tragedy, as
Edwin Berry Burgum points out, is not a result of an
implacable nemesis wreaking vengeance on an ungov-
ernable pride.[2] Rather is it a kind of final irony that
once they have come to a recognition of themselves

and a realization of the world that made them, they are destroyed physically. Yet their "short happy lives" have not been lived in vain; the vision of a humanity at peace with itself and free to explore its potentialities completes the tone of Wright's short stories.

There is a thematic progression in these stories, each of which deals with the Negro's struggle for survival and freedom. In the first story, flight is described —and here Wright is at his artistic best, fashioning his taut, spare prose to the movements and thoughts of the fugitive. In "Big Boy Leaves Home," four truant adolescent boys are discovered naked by a white woman as they trespass in a swimming hole forbidden to Negroes. The woman's escort kills two of them, but the other two manage to overcome him and kill him. The narrative now centers on Big Boy, the leader of the group, who flees home, and is advised by the leaders of the Negro community (that is, the deacons of the Negro church) to conceal himself in a kiln on the hills outside of town until morning when a truck driver will pick him up and drive him to Chicago. The boy manages to scramble in the dark to the hiding place, and while there views the brutal burning of his comrade who had escaped with him. The following morning the Negro truck driver arrives and Big Boy escapes.

The pathos of the story lies in the precariousness of the lives of the Negro community. The story opens on an American dream setting—an idyllic country atmosphere—carrying echoes of Mark Twain and *Peck's Bad Boy* as the four boys push, jostle, wrestle, joke, and sing their way to the swimming hole. But the results of their joy and zest are the death of three of the boys, the destruction of Big Boy's house and Big Boy's lonely flight to the big city. Hence Wright sets up a situation whose simplicity and innocence ring a nostalgic appeal in the reader—and then jars the reader into a sense of horror when he comes to realize what such a situation can mean if Negroes are involved. For Big

Boy and his friends are not merely simple, unassuming fellows with picturesque ways of expressing themselves. They are bawdy and vulgar; they tell inane jokes; they are neither committed nor uncommitted to a way of life; they are aware only of themselves and the limits of their own pleasure. Their fate is moving not because they are extraordinary, but because they are so commonplace. To be sure Big Boy is a cut above his companions, yet despite his developing maturity, at the moment of truth he remains a boy—and there is a skillful interplay of the boy-man aspects of Big Boy's character (perhaps his name is significant) in the latter part of the story.

Wright is particularly good at depicting terror and Big Boy's changing reactions to his situation not only by means of interior monologue but by describing Big Boy's movements as well. When, for example, Big Boy arrives at the kiln, he discovers he must first kill a snake that has ensconced itself in the depths of the pit. Somehow the startling confrontation with the snake and the methodical, impassioned manner in which Big Boy destroys it suggest at one and the same time his terror and burning hatred of the whites. Later, now safely in the hole himself, he fantasies killing whites in just the same way as he killed the snake—whipping them, stamping on them, and kicking their heads against the sand. His dreams of glory— an ironic comment on the usual order of boys' fantasies—are headlines in which he imagines himself described as the killer of twenty white lynchers.

Although "Big Boy" is a relatively long story, the rhythm of events is swift, and the time consumed from beginning to end is less than twenty-four hours. The prose is correspondingly fashioned to meet the pace of the plot. The story is divided into five parts, each of which constitutes a critical episode in Big Boy's progress from idyll, through violence, to misery, terror, and escape. As the tension mounts, Wright employs more and more of a terse and taut declaratory prose, fraught with overtones and meanings unspoken —reminiscent vaguely of the early Hemingway.

> Will pushed back a square trapdoor [of the truck] which swung above the back of the driver's seat. Big Boy pulled through, landing with a thud on the bottom. On hands and knees he looked around in the semi-darkness.
> "Wheres Bobo?"
> Big Boy stared.
> "Wheres Bobo?"
> "They got im."
> "When?"
> "Las night."
> "The mob?"
> Big Boy pointed in the direction of a charred sapling on the slope of the opposite hill. Will looked. The trapdoor fell. The engine purred, the gears whined, and the truck lurched forward over the muddy road, sending Big Boy on his side.[3]

Big Boy's escape was effected through the will of the oppressed Negro community despite obvious risks. Wright's concept of this community—extending beyond the Negro world—clasping hands with its white oppressed brothers, informs the very essence of a developing social vision in the other stories of *Uncle Tom's Children*. And though Wright's world falls far short of ever fulfilling this vision, the dream lives on ironically stronger with every tragic failure of his heroes to realize their humanity.

"Down by the Riverside," the next story in the collection, is not nearly so successful. If flight (as represented by "Big Boy Leaves Home") is one aspect of the Negro's struggle for survival in the South, Christian humility, forbearance, courage, and stoic endurance are the themes of Wright's second piece. But here the plot becomes too contrived; coincidence is piled upon coincidence, and the inevitability of his protagonist's doom does not ring quite true. The story relates the odyssey of Brother Mann, his pregnant wife, small son, and mother-in-law, who set out in a stolen boat at a time when the Mississippi is overflowing its banks, drowning villages and farms—in order to find a Red Cross hospital where his wife can safely deliver her child. One of the houses he passes on his perilous trek is owned by the proprietor (Heartfield) of the stolen boat, who tries to kill him. Mann, in self defense, shoots back and kills Heartfield. When later he arrives at the hospital, he learns that his wife is dead. He is next separated from his son and mother-in-law and conscripted to set sandbags on the levee. When the levees break down, he is sent back to the hospital, where he is put to work aiding the survivors to escape. Afterwards he is put on a small boat with another Negro to search for people who might still be inhabiting their floating homes. The first house to which he is sent belongs to none other than Heartfield whose son and wife recognize him as the killer. Mann considers killing them, but the course of events changes his mind and he ultimately rescues them. When they reach the safety of the hills, the Heartfields tell the white citizenry who he is, and he is shot.

Despite the virtuosity of Wright's prose style which lends a certain plausibility to Mann's adventures, the plot is overladen with events and symbols that appear to foreshadow Mann's doom. Brother Mann (the name is obviously symbolic), along with the others in the family sings "Down by the Riverside," at his wife's bedside just prior to their journey. Although the song rings an ironic counterpart to what happens to Mann later, the words are hardly appropriate to the occasion ("Ahm gonna lay down mah sword n shiel / Down by the riverside / Ah ain gonna study war no mo.") That Mann's boat should float past Heartfield's house is perhaps a legitimate turn of the events but that the Heartfields would recognize Mann in the darkness on the raging waters is stretching credibility. Again, that

Mann should later be sent to Heartfield's home to rescue the family strikes one as contrived, as does the occasion when Mann, axe in hand, prepared to kill the family, is prevented from doing so by a sudden tilting of the house on the waters which throws him off balance. Finally, that the Heartfields should turn him in as a murderer without making some extenuating comments about him as their rescuer seems almost unbelievable even for the most rabid Mississippi white racist.

Yet, there is a certain epic quality to the piece—man steadily pursuing his course against a malevolent nature, only to be cut down later by the ingratitude of his fellow men—that is suggestive of Twain or Faulkner. And Mann's long-suffering perseverance and stubborn will to survive endow him with a rare mythic Biblical quality. Wright even structures his story like a Biblical chronicle, in five brief episodes, each displaying in its way Mann's humble courage against his fate. But if Mann's simple Christian virtues failed to save him, it was in part because the ground had not yet been laid on which these virtues might flourish. The recognition that the bourgeois ethic is incapable of providing men with the possibility of fulfilling themselves is an element of Wright's next story.

The plot of "Long Black Song" is relatively simple. A white travelling salesman seduces a young Negro farm mother (Sarah) whose husband has gone to the town to buy provisions. When Silas returns home, he discovers her betrayal and attempts to whip her. She flees, but steals quietly back to recover her infant. The following day the salesman returns with a white friend. Silas horsewhips one and kills the other. Later, Sarah, watching from a distance observes a posse of lynchers burn down the house in which Silas has entrenched himself, but not before he has succeeded in killing one or two others. The success of the story,

perhaps Wright's best, lies in the successful integra-
tion of plot, imagery, and character which echo the
tragic theme of Silas's doomed awareness of himself
and the inadequacy of the bourgeois values by which
he has been attempting to live. Silas's recognition is
his death knell, but he achieves a dignity in death that
he had never known in life. His sexual jealousies
arouse his long repressed burning racial enmities, and
he comes to realize that the sacrifices he has been
making for the past ten years to buy his own farm are
all meaningless in the face of a scale of values that
allows for the selfish exploitation and manipulation of
people. The caste system has made the bourgeois
dream of owning his own farm impossible, and he is
made to see the wider implications of his own life. For
the past ten years he has been living an illusion; the
denial of human dignity in race relations renders freedom and independence unattainable in any sphere of
human activities.

> 'The white folks ain never gimme a chance. They
> ain never give no black man a chance! There ain
> nothin in yo whole life yuh kin keep from em! They
> take you lan! They take yo freedom! They take you
> women! N then they take yo life.' [4]

When he decides to fight it out, he is determined, at
least, to become the master of his own death. Silas is
more wordly, less instinctive than his wife. Steeped as
he is in middle-class values, he regards his wife as his
personal property and the sanctity of marriage as in-
violable. Yet when his revelation comes, he achieves
truly tragic stature.

It is Sarah, though, who is the most memorable
portrayal in the story. The narrative unfolds from her
point of view—and she becomes, at the end, a kind of
deep mother earth character, registering her primal
instincts and reactions to the violence and senselessness she sees all about her. But for all that, she remains beautifully human—her speech patterns and

thoughts responding to an inner rhythm, somehow out of touch with the foolish strivings of men, yet caught up in her own melancholy memories and desires. As she moves through her lonely day she remembers Tom, her former lover, now gone from her in the war (the time is just after World War I), the only person whom she had ever really loved. Wright conveys her mood and memories and vagaries of character in sensuous color imagery—while certain cadences suggest perhaps Gertrude Stein whom Wright regarded as one of his chief influences. (Indeed "Melanctha" may have been the prototype of Sarah.) Later as she is being seduced by the salesman, Wright fuses images of the seasons, the days and nights, the lush colors, and the earth rhythm into a condensed and brilliant evocation of her nature.

> A liquid metal covered her and she rode on the curve of white bright days and dark black nights and the surge of the long gladness of summer and the ebb of the deep dream of sleep in winter till a high red wave of hotness drowned her in a deluge of silver and blue that boiled her blood and blistered her *flesh bangbang-bang.*[5]

Sarah is Wright's most lyrical achievement, and Silas, her husband, Wright's most convincing figure of redemption. Yet Silas's redemption is at best a private affair—and the Negro's plight is no better as a result of his determination to fight his oppressors with their own weapons. He is hopelessly outnumbered. A recognition that the white and black oppressed share a common human heritage is the theme of Wright's next story.

"Fire and Cloud" takes place during the Depression and deals with the efforts of a Negro minister, the Reverend Taylor, to acquire food relief for the near starving Negro community of a medium sized southern town. For some reason, not made altogether clear, the white civic leaders have been refusing help and a protest march is being planned (a number of poor whites are expected to participate) in order to make them change their minds. The march, significantly, is being organized by two Communists, a white and a Negro, who hope to persuade Taylor to join them in sponsoring the demonstration. Meanwhile the mayor, who has granted Taylor some favors in the past, the police chief, and Lowe, the chief of the industrial squad (an anti-Communist committee, presumably) are putting pressure on the minister to dissuade his followers from marching. Although Taylor refuses to sponsor the parade, he says he will march with his parishioners if they wish him to do so. The night before the demonstration is to take place, he is kidnapped by a group of whites and brutally horsewhipped. Instead of breaking Taylor's will, the lashing serves to inspire him with a new vision. God's will can best be realized by mass social action. The demonstration on an integrated basis takes place with Taylor leading his followers. The Mayor, observing its success, relents and promises the poor their food.

Although "Fire and Cloud" won Wright the *Story* magazine prize, it is the weakest piece in the collection. Wright too often resorts to stereotype. The individual whites in imagery and fact are all of one piece —icy, cold, hard, and malevolent; the blacks, simple, unassuming, trusting and God-fearing, but driven to their desperate actions by the hunger they feel in their bodies. Even the black Judas in their midst, the Deacon Smith, who sides with the white authorities, is motivated only by his desire to take the Reverend Taylor's place as minister of the church. The story line itself, divided into thirteen separate sections, tracing Taylor's spiritual growth from passive Christian resignation to active social participation, resembles the standard plot structure of proletarian fiction of the 1930's—downtrodden, humbled "bottomdogs" perceiving through the course of their experiences a vision of a new and better world. Taylor's socialist vision is couched in Biblical allusions, but remains, nonetheless, true to form. "Gawd ain no lie! His eyes grew wet with tears blurring his vision; the sky trembled; the buildings wavered as if about to topple; and the earth shook." Taylor cries out exultingly, "Freedom belongs to the strong." [6]

Yet despite the clichés surrounding his character, there is an authentic ring to the minister's driving ambition to be the Moses of his people. And Wright records with consummate skill the way in which he evokes responses from his congregation. Taylor's self-assumed Biblical role allows him to see perhaps better than any of Wright's previous heroes that Negro freedom depends upon Christian brotherhood. Moreover, as leader of the Negro community, he perceives that success requires that he organize mass social action. He cautions his son who, like Silas of "Long Black Song," wants to resort to the same kind of isolated violence that whites use against Negroes.

> We gotta git wid the *people*, son. Too long we done tried t do this thing our way n when we failed we wanted t run out n pay-off the white folks. Then they kill us up like flies.[7]

Wright's treatment of the relationship between the white power structure and bourgeois Negro leadership in southern cities is a theme he would develop in greater detail in his last published novel, *The Long Dream*. But it is interesting to note that Wright here for the first time reveals the extent of the corruption and moral blackmail involved. Insofar as Taylor had been acquiescent and accommodating, the white civic authorities tolerated him and even recognized him as a fine leader of his people. When Taylor discovers that he had been manipulated all along to suit their own purposes, he is beaten and discarded. Taylor's discovery that the "cordial" relationships that exist between the white and Negro communities are based ultimately on an underlying reality of terror and brute power is a key theme of *The Long Dream*. But unfortunately in *The Long Dream*, the only alternative to submitting to this humiliation is flight whereas in "Fire and Cloud" Taylor's Negroes demonstrate, protest, and succeed. It would seem that Wright had his chronology confused. In 1938 when "Fire and Cloud" was published, any Negro protest movement would have been bloodily suppressed. By 1958, the time of *The Long Dream*, the first stirrings of the Negro rebellion had already begun to achieve results. Ironically, Wright had given up hope in a dream he had visualized so accurately twenty years before.

Wright progresses from the idea of organized Negro-white protest to the specific idea of a society based on Marxist principles. Although the two chief characters of "Bright and Morning Star" are cruelly maimed and murdered, they die secure in the belief that the cause for which they had given up their lives will some day be realized. In some respects "Bright and Morning Star" is the most classical of Wright's tragedies inasmuch as Wright's scapegoats die not in vain, but for an orderly, healthy, and progressive society that will flourish as a result of their death.

The story is related in the third person from the point of view of an elderly Negro tenant farmer's widow whose two sons (one of whom is already in jail) are Communist Party organizers. As the story opens, Sue reminisces about the hardships she has undergone in her life and how her two sons have managed to convert her simple Christian beliefs of a heaven in the next world to a vision of a Communist utopia on earth. In effect, the transition was not hard for her to make, since the principles underlying her old faith are the same as those of Communism. She discovers herself humming an old hymn, "Bright and Morning Star," the star signalling the new era approaching with the Resurrection. Reva, the white daughter of a tenant farmer, who loves her son, Johnny Boy, calls on her and tells her that the sheriff and other white officials have learned of a secret Party meeting that is to be held the following evening. When Johnny-Boy returns later that evening, Sue delivers Reva's message and Johnny-Boy goes out in the rain to warn the other Party members. Shortly after Johnny-Boy's departure, the sheriff and his men break into her house and demand to know the whereabouts of her son. When she refuses to tell them, they beat her and leave. A new Party member, Booker (white) arrives (whom she distrusts instinctively) and tells her Johnny-Boy has been captured. Booker manages to get from her the names of the other Party members. Reva returns and tells her that Booker is an informer. Sue now determines to kill Booker before he can give the names to the sheriff. She takes a short cut through the woods to the place where Johnny-Boy lies bound, tortured, and mutilated by the sheriff and his men. When Booker arrives on the scene, she shoots him before he can speak, whereupon she and Johnny-Boy are shot and killed.

The story is remarkable for the intense religious fervor that informs Sue's character. Like the Reverend Taylor of "Fire and Cloud," she conceives her mission in Biblical apocalyptic terms. But here the imagery is of a higher order, the metaphors sustained in a mounting tension until an ultimate sublimity is reached that transports her suffering into a mystical unity. As she lies dying,

> Focused and pointed she was, buried in the depths of her star, swallowed in its peace and strength; and not feeling her flesh growing cold, cold as the rain that fell from the invisible sky upon the doomed living and the dead that never dies.[8]

Like the other pieces in *Uncle Tom's Children,* "Bright and Morning Star" celebrates southern Negro folk whose faith, courage, and endurance Wright regarded as easily translatable, in terms of constructive social action, with the new dispensation of Communism. Yet Wright's Negroes achieve their sense of recognition through the course of their Negro experiences, and not through any inculcation of Communist ideals. As has been already shown, Taylor and Sue arrive at their decisions as a result of their peculiar Negro folk mysticism—or, perhaps, as Wright would have it, a native Negro revolutionism. Even Sue is a Negro first, before she is a Communist. Although she presumably possesses maternal feelings toward the white girl who loves her son, she has an instinctive distrust of whites. She tells her son that the Judas among them must be a white man, and although he chides her for being a black chauvinist, her Negro instincts prove truer than his Communist training.

Hence, Wright's militant Negroes, despite their protestations to the contrary, often sound more like black nationalists than Communist internationalists. It was perhaps this facet of Wright's work, in addition to the obvious, extreme, and frequent isolated individualism of his heroes that had now begun to disturb Communist Party officials. Yet regardless of whether Wright had been at heart a Communist, an outsider, or a nationalist when he wrote these pieces, there can be little doubt that they draw a good deal of their dramatic strength from the black and white world Wright saw. There is little the reader can do but sympathize with Wright's Negroes and loathe and despise the whites. There are no shadings, ambiguities, few psychological complexities. But these are of course the weaknesses of the stories as well.

How then account for their overall success? First of all, they *are* stories. Wright is a story teller and his plots are replete with conflict, incident, and suspense. Secondly, Wright is a stylist. He has an unerring "feel" for dialogue, his narrations are controlled in terse, tense rhythms, and he manages to communicate mood, atmosphere, and character in finely worked passages of lyric intensity. But above all they are stories whose sweep and magnitude are suffused with their author's impassioned convictions about the dignity of man, and a profound pity for the degraded, the poor and oppressed who, in the face of casual brutality, cling obstinately to their humanity.

Eight Men is a posthumous miscellany of eight of Wright's prose pieces that had not previously been collected in book form.[9] Two of the stories had been written in the thirties, three in the forties, and three in the fifties. One of the pieces, "The Man Who Went to Chicago," is in reality part of an unpublished chapter of *Black Boy*. Although *Eight Men* appeared two months after Wright died, it is clear that its publication was no hasty attempt to take advantage of any publicity occasioned by his death. Wright himself had evidently been preparing the book for some time and had anticipated its publication by dedicating it to friends he had made in Paris. Unlike the pieces in *Uncle Tom's Children*, these stories are not arranged along any progressively thematic lines; instead the order in which they are assembled indicates that Wright was more concerned with showing a variety of styles, settings and points of view. To be sure, they all deal in one way or another with Negro oppression, but they do not point, as Wright's previous collection of stories did, to any specific social conclusion. With one exception—"The Man Who Lived Underground"— they are considerably shorter than the pieces in *Uncle Tom's Children*, and since they represent Wright's work over a far greater span of years, the uneven quality of some of his writing becomes more apparent.

Wright did not particularly mature as a craftsman although he experimented more in the forties and fifties trying to find appropriate prose forms to suit his post-Communist intellectual growth. The stories in *Eight Men* are representative of the different stages of Wright's development. The pieces that he had written in the thirties ("The Man Who Saw The Flood,"

"The Man Who Was Almost A Man") deal with oppressed southern Negro peasants; the stories of the forties ("The Man Who Lived Underground," "The Man Who Went to Chicago," "The Man Who Killed A Shadow") employ an urban setting to depict the Negro's "invisibility," outsider, or underground status; the stories of the fifties ("Man of All Work," "Man, God Ain't Like That," "Big Black Good Man") celebrate in an odd sort of way a kind of Negro nationalism—Negro virility as opposed to the white man's flabbiness, and a proud awareness of an African identity. In the latter period too there appears now an element of humor—albeit sometimes strained or ironic—and a lessening of the fierce tensions that had characterized his fiction up until this time. These changes do not necessarily reveal any slackening in Wright's commitment to Negro equality, but they do suggest that he may perhaps have now discovered himself in the process of acquiring a more even emotional equilibrium. Possibly the success of African independence movements for which he had so long fought encouraged him to believe that a turning point in race relationships had been achieved. Whatever the reasons, the hard narrative drive of Wright's earlier work is no longer present—the stories are now more psychological, more sophisticated, perhaps even more self-consciously stories. Yet somehow one feels that these are transition pieces, that Wright was moving in a new direction toward new subject matter and new themes—and that possibly he might have found what he was looking for, had he not died so young.

"The Man Who Saw The Flood," the first of the stories in *Eight Men*, was published initially in 1938 in *New Masses* under the title, "Silt." The piece is little more than a vignette—possibly intended as a sketch for a longer story-dealing with a tenant farm family of three who return to their devastated home after a flood. Wright best evokes their sense of loss and desolation by images. As they slosh silently across their oozey floors, they observe their dresser sitting "cater-cornered its drawers and sides bulging like a bloated corpse. The bed with the mattress still on it, was like a giant casket forged of mud. Two smashed chairs lay in a corner, as though huddled together for protection." [10]

Wright's other story of the thirties—a far more developed piece—was first published in *Harper's Bazaar* in 1939 under the title, "Almos' A Man." It is less sensationally dramatic than Wright's other Depression pieces in that the confrontation between whites and blacks is not nearly so violent. But it may be for this very reason that the point Wright is making about the ravages of the caste system is all the more telling. For the story speaks not simply of the economic exploitation of the southern Negro, but how this exploitation affects the psyche of an adolescent Negro boy. What makes this theme particularly effective is that the boy is not especially complex or sensitive; he is neither "socially aware" nor is he like Big Boy, a leader among boys of his age. Yet it is through the relative naïveté of his nature that the reader becomes cognizant of the terrible conditions of his life.

"The Man Who Was Almost A Man" tells the story of sixteen-year-old Dave who works in the fields and dreams of owning his own gun. The gun evidently symbolizes for him self-respect, virility, strength, all of which attributes Dave sorely lacks. The other Negro field hands taunt him, his father frequently beats him, and his mother receives his wages directly from Dave's white employer, Mr. Hawkins. One evening Dave manages to persuade his mother to allow him to buy an antiquated pistol from a white storekeeper—and the following morning Dave accidentally shoots Mr. Hawkins' mule. When he is discovered, he learns that he must work two years for Mr. Hawkins in order to pay for the dead animal. Rather than submit to this final outrage, he jumps aboard a passing train travelling north—his gun still securely in his pocket.

The pathos of the story lies in the poverty of Dave's

dreams. For him, as for most adolescents, manhood is the highest order of achievement—but his paucity of social and emotional experience makes him view that goal in the image of a gun. It is clear from the very beginning of the story that Dave feels himself emasculated not only by his parents and peers, but by the very conditions of his work. Hence the killing of the mule may not have been so accidental as Dave had supposed. On the one hand he may be killing the mule in himself that has been submitting to all these assaults on his dignity—at a certain point in the story Dave in a fit of pique calls himself a mule—and on the other hand he may be striking out at his white employer by destroying his property. Significantly, once the accident has occurred Dave feels free to express his hatred in fantasies of killing the white man. In any event, he is now capable of acting, of making a decision—even if the decision is to flee rather than give up his gun to his father. It is instructive to note in this respect that the general pattern of plot and action in "Almost A Man" anticipates a similar pattern in Wright's novel, *Native Son*, that would be published later the same year. In the novel, the accidental killing of a white girl gives the murderer a sense of freedom and manhood he had never known before. Like the pieces in *Uncle Tom's Children*, much of the narrative is carried chiefly by dialogue and interior monologue. This is the last fictional work employing a southern setting that Wright would publish until his Mississippi novel eighteen years later. This story too marks the end of one phase of Wright's development.

The only significant work of fiction Wright produced in the decade of the forties was his long story, "The Man Who Lived Underground." (*Native Son* although published in 1940 had been completed the previous year.) The history of the publication of "Underground Man" offers a suggestive link between Wright's Marxist social views and his metaphysical speculations. Originally published in *Accent* (Spring

1942) as two excerpts from a novel, Wright published a considerably fuller version in Edwin Seaver's *Cross-section* two years later. In the two year interval Wright had broken with the Communist Party and had intensified his interests in philosophy and Freudian psychology. It is of course not possible to know all the changes Wright had made between 1942 and 1944—but there appears to be less emphasis on social injustice in the latter version. The ultimate impression one carries away is not merely that of social protest, but rather protest against the nature of man, the human condition—what Camus called the metaphysical protest.

The 1944 version becomes essentially a detailed expansion of Wright's earlier piece. A Negro, Fred Daniels, in flight from the police who have falsely accused him of murder, descends through a manhole on the street into a sewer. Sloshing his way through the slime and sewage of the city, he discovers an entrance to the basement of a building adjacent to the sewer. Here he finds tools, and ultimately manages to dig his way through the walls of other buildings adjacent to the sewer. In the course of his underground expeditions he visits a Negro church, an undertaker's embalming room, a movie, a butcher's shop, a radio shop, and a jewelry store. He plunders whatever strikes his fancy (watches, diamonds, a butcher cleaver, a gun, a radio, and money) and brings these back to the secret room he had discovered in one of the buildings. He finds too that, from an invisible vantage point, he can view the nefarious behavior of respectable people who imagine they are acting unobserved. He comes to understand that the nether world in which he dwells is the real world of the human heart—and that the surface world which hums above him in the streets of the city is senseless and meaningless—a kind of unreality which men project to hide from themselves the awful blackness of their souls. He is invested suddenly with a sense of pity for all mankind. All men are guilty; it does not matter whether or not he killed the woman about whom he was forced to confess. He was guilty nonetheless by virtue of his being human. He rises Lazarus-like to the surface of the city to announce his message. Charged with the zeal of a prophet, he runs first to a church where the choir is ironically chanting a hymn quite opposed to the truth he now knows:

> Oh, wondrous sight upon the cross
> Vision sweet and divine
> Oh, wondrous sight upon the cross
> Full of such love sublime

He is turned away as being disreputable. He goes next to the police from whom he had fled. They tell him that they have found the real murderer, and that he is free—but he insists on his guilt. They regard him as deranged. He leads them to the sewer in which he had been hiding, plunges in once again, and asks them to follow. But one policeman, fearing some sort of trick, shoots him, and he is swept away dead in the scummy waters that flow below the city.

No mere synopsis can do justice to the story. Here Wright is at his storytelling best, dealing with subject matter he handles best—the terrified fugitive in flight from his pursuers. Like Wright's other fugitives, Fred Daniels exercises a kind of instinct for survival that he perhaps never knew he possessed. But what makes him different from the others is that he is not merely a victim of a racist society, but that he has become by the very nature of his experiences a symbol of all men in that society—the pursuers and the pursued. For what the underground man has learned in his sewer is that all men carry about in their hearts an underground man who determines their behavior and attitudes in the aboveground world. The underground man is the essential nature of all men—and is composed of dread, terror, and guilt. Here then lies the essential difference between Wright's Communist and post-Communist period. Heretofore dread, terror, and guilt had been the lot of the Negro in a world that had thrust upon him the role of a despised inferior. Now they are the attributes of all mankind. Previously Wright's Negro protagonists had been required to discover their own values, build their own ethics in a world that denied them access to "white" morality. In a word, white denial of Negro freedom rendered the Negro free to seek his identity outside the standards of the white world. But now these standards are held to be as illusory for whites as they had always been inaccessible for Negroes. All of men's striving, activities, and ideals are simply a means of keeping from themselves the knowledge of their underground nature. When Fred Daniels attempts to educate men to this truth, he is shot and killed. The police officer who kills him says, "You've got to shoot this kind. They'd wreck things." [11] In reality what Wright is doing is transferring what he once regarded as a special Negro experience, a special Negro truth in white America, to all men, white and Negro, everywhere. If Negroes are more aware of this truth, it is because their outsider-pariah status has made it less easy for them to delude themselves.

Fred Daniels is then Everyman, and his story is very nearly a perfect modern allegory. The Negro who lives in the underground of the city amidst its sewage and slime is not unlike the creature who dwells amidst the sewage of the human heart. And Fred Daniels knows that all of the ways men attempt to persuade themselves that their lives are meaningful and rational are delusions. As he stands over his loot of the above-ground world in his darkened room, he realizes these "images with their tongueless reality were striving to tell him something." What he discovers at bottom is that all men are murderous and in love with death. Significantly Fred places a butcher's bloody meat cleaver next to a "forest" of green paper dollar bills he had earlier pasted on all his walls. But paradoxically despite Fred's new found knowledge of the savagery of the human heart and the meaninglessness of the above-ground world, he recognizes its instinctive appeal as well, and he must absurdly rise to the surface once more.

It is understandable how in 1944 young French existentialist authors must have seen in Wright's works a confirmation of their own views. The dread, the terror, the guilt, the nausea had always been basic thematic elements in Wright's fiction—and now in "The Man Who Lived Underground," they are made the explicit components of the human personality. Like Wright's heroes, the characters of existentialist authors move about in a world devoid of principles, God, and purpose—and suffer horror at their awesome godlike powers as they create their own personalities and values out of the chaos of existence. But in some respects Wright's heroes are different. They are alienated often enough not from any intellectually reasoned position (at this stage in Wright's career), but by chance happenings in their lives or an accident of birth—race, for example. (In Fred Daniels' case, for instance, he is a Negro who quite by chance happened to be near the scene of a crime.) They arrive then accidentally at their insights, and as a result of having discovered themselves outside the rules of conventional social behavior recognize that they are free to shape (and are therefore responsible for) their own lives. But this is not primarily why they suffer guilt. Wright seems to prefer a Freudian explanation; guilt is instinctively connected with the trauma of birth.

> Why was this sense of guilt so seemingly innate, so easy to come by, to think, to feel, so verily physical? It seemed that when one felt this guilt one was retracing in one's feelings a faint pattern designed long before; it seemed that one was always trying to remember a gigantic shock that had left a haunting impression upon one's body which one could not forget or shake off, but which had been forgotten by the conscious mind, creating in one's life a state of eternal anxiety.[12]

Hence, for Wright, a man's freedom is circumscribed by his very humanity. In ways he cannot possibly control, his nature or "essence" precedes his existence. But however different the routes French existentialist authors and Wright may have taken, they meet on common ground in regard to their thrilled horror at man's rootlessness—at the heroism of his absurd striving.

"The Man Who Lived Underground" undoubtedly owes something in the way of plot and theme to *Les Miserables,* and to what Camus called the "Dostoevskian experience of the condemned man"—but, above all, Fred Daniels' adventures suggest something of Wright's own emotions after ten years in the Communist underground. The air of bitterness, the almost strident militancy are gone—momentarily at least—and in their place a compassion and despair—compassion for man trapped in his underground nature and despair that he will ever be able to set himself free.

Wright's two other representations of the forties are partial reflections of "Underground Man." "The Man Who Went to Chicago" is interesting because Wright here has chosen to depict himself living literally in an underground situation. One of Wright's first jobs after coming to Chicago was that of a hospital attendant. He had a number of menial tasks—one of which took him to the hospital basement to feed caged animals on whom certain experimental inoculations were being performed. On one occasion two of the other Negro attendants with whom Wright worked began to fight, and in the course of their quarrel pushed against and fell among some of the cages, thereby setting free some of the animals. The resulting chaos of violence, animals, and men in the cluttered basement comes to symbolize the true heartbeat of the civilization in which the hospital stands as such a deceptive example.

"The Man Who Killed A Shadow" was the first of Wright's works to be published after he had gone to Paris.[13] The story, which in some ways hearkens back to *Native Son*, deals with a Negro who inadvertently kills a white woman. The woman in this case is a forty year old, sexually repressed, white librarian who commands the Negro to look at her legs. When he tries to flee, she screams and he brutally hacks her to death for fear of being discovered alone with her. What makes the story something other than a restatement of the Bigger Thomas theme is Wright's use of the Negro as a symbol of libidinal abandon. The irony, of course, lies in the fact that Saul Saunders is as much a shadow of a man as the woman he kills is a shadow of a woman. Like the underground man he lives on a plane of fear, guilt, and dread. Hence the Negro man and white woman are not only shadows to one another, but shadows to themselves.

The fifties saw Wright experimenting with new subject matter and new forms. Problems of race remain the central issue, but are now dealt with from changing perspectives. For the first time there are two stories with non-American settings, and race neurosis is treated more as the white man's dilemma than as the black man's burden. This shift in emphasis from black to white is accompanied by corresponding shifts in social viewpoint. Racial antagonisms do not appear to be immediately—or for that matter remotely—traceable to compelling class interests. It is clear that Wright was trying to broaden the range and scope of his fiction—that he was trying to move away somewhat from the psyche of the oppressed Negro peasant or proletariat toward characters of varying social and ethnic backgrounds. The three novels Wright produced in this ten year period bear out this conclusion. In the first, *The Outsider* (1953), he wrote of his hero that though a Negro "he could have been of any race." *Savage Holiday*, written the following year, contains no Negro characters and deals with the misfortunes of a white, "respectable" middle-aged retired insurance executive. *The Long Dream* (1957) is written from the point of view of an adolescent, middle-class Negro boy.

Wright was apparently reaching for a universality he felt he had not yet achieved—but his craft was not quite equal to the tasks he had set for himself. Too often, as before, his whites appear as stereotypes, and his Negroes are a bit too noble or innocent. In the 1930's Wright's social vision lent his stories an air of conviction, a momentum all their own; in the 1950's Wright's quieter catholicity, his wider intellectuality, perhaps removed his stories from this kind of cumulative dread tension, the sense of urgency, that made his earlier works so immediately gripping.

Nonetheless it cannot be said that Wright's new stories do not possess their own narrative qualities. Two of the stories are written entirely in dialogue with no interceding explanatory prose passages. This kind of dramatic framework has, of course, certain advantages. For one thing, pace is considerably accelerated, and the climactic confrontations are made more immediately suspenseful—if perhaps somewhat less meaningful than in the *Uncle Tom* stories. What these stories sorely lack are the charged, vibrant rhythms and vivid lyric imagery that so rounded out character and theme in his earlier works. Perhaps Wright wanted to pare his prose down to what he regarded as bare essentials—just as he may have fancied his idol, Gertrude Stein, had done. Whatever the reasons, the results are only occasionally successful.

"Man of All Work," probably composed in 1953, was inspired by an item Wright read in *Jet* about a man who dressed himself as a woman in order to find work as a domestic. In a sense this story appears to develop more fully an idea first implied in "The Man Who Killed A Shadow"—that racial antagonisms are related in some fashion to serious sexual maladjustment. Wright builds his case carefully, playing delicately but never explicitly with notions of homosexuality, transvestism, castration, and hermaphroditism. The story—the first of Wright's dialogue pieces—deals with a Negro man who informs his wife that their

situation is so desperate that he intends to dress himself in his wife's clothes and seek employment as a
maid. She protests, but he persists—and shortly thereafter finds himself working for a white family, the
Fairchilds. It soon develops that, among his other
duties (cooking, cleaning and taking care of a small
child) Carl must stave off the predatory advances of
Mr. Fairchild, who apparently regards all Negro maids
as fair game. At one juncture Mrs. Fairchild enters
while the two men are wrestling and becomes so jealous that she shoots hysterically at her husband's presumed paramour. When it is discovered that Carl is
after all a man—and not very seriously wounded—they
pay him two months wages and make him promise
that he will not tell the authorities of Mrs. Fairchild's
attempt at murder.

The story unfolds in three swiftly changing scenes:
Carl's home, the Fairchild's house, and back again to
Carl's home. All the reader knows of character and
action is what he can infer from the dialogue. The
dialogue itself sounds occasionally stiff and awkward,
especially when Wright attempts to relate what the
characters are doing at a particular moment, or what
events have just taken place. (There is some evidence
Wright had written this piece as a radio play which
may in part explain the awkward transitions.) The
story (or play) makes a grim little joke about mis-
taken identity on several levels. Because Carl cannot
provide for his wife and children, he has symbolically
been denied his virility long before he actually decides
to appropriate the role of the woman. The Fairchilds,
perhaps significantly named, also undergo a similar
confusion of sexual roles. It is obvious from the moment Carl applies for the job that Mrs. Fairchild plays
the dominant part in her relationship to her husband.
She makes it clear to Carl (who calls himself Lucy)
that she regards her husband as an irresponsible child,
particularly when he drinks. Perhaps because of the
brusque efficient way in which she runs her family, she

has, in her way, emasculated her husband, who attempts to recover his virility in drink and Negro girls. To compound the confusion the Fairchild's little girl dominates both her parents in this white, child-centered middle-class family. The final confusion lies in the way whites look at the Negro woman as a figure both of a wild physical abandon and warm motherhood. Poor Carl-Lucy, whom American culture has effectively deprived of his sexuality, is expected to play both roles—and it is in the role of the latter, as mammy-nurse, that Wright produces one rather good ironic twist. In what amounts to a parody of Red Riding Hood, the frightening little girl cross-examines her disguised nursemaid.

> —Lucy, your arms are so big.
> —Hunh?
> —And there's so much hair on them.
> —Oh, that's nothing.
> —And you've got so many big muscles.
> —Oh, that comes from washing and cleaning and cooking. Lifting heavy pots and pans.
> —And your voice is not at all like Bertha's.
> —What do you mean?
> —Your voice is heavy, like a man's.
> —Oh, that's from singing so much, child.
> —And you hold your cigarette in your mouth like Papa holds his, with one end dropping down.
> —Hunh? Oh, that's because my hands are busy, child.[14]

Wright's other dialogue piece, "Man, God Ain't Like That," although more ambitious in that it treats of European-African relationships, is not nearly so successful or clever.[15] There are a number of reasons, but the principal one is that Wright has attempted to impose in fictional form his rather complex ideas about the psychology of imperialism. Or, put another way, plot and action issue from Wright's preconceptions about Europeans and Africans in certain situations rather than from the actual characters and situations he writes about. The story opens with a description of a journey an English painter and his wife are making through the back country of the Ashanti. John, the artist, feels that he can somehow reinvigorate himself in a primitive setting. In the course of their travels they adopt as their servant a queerly religious Ashanti boy who sings Methodist hymns publicly, but makes strange secret sacrifices to his dead ancestors when he is alone. John regards Babu as an amusing curiosity and takes him with him to Paris. Babu, who adores his white master, is overwhelmingly impressed by his civilization and disappears for a time presumably observing the sights of Paris. He returns to his master's apartment just as John is preparing to leave for a gallery that will be displaying his African paintings for the first time. Babu is convinced that John is Christ and that he, Babu, must kill him. He reasons that since white men had to kill their god to achieve such a magnificent civilization, so Babu must kill his master to achieve the same results. The artist pleads with him—but to no avail; Babu proceeds sanguinely about his task. The scene shifts to two Paris detectives who are discovered discussing a baffling murder that had occurred some five years before. They are convinced that John must have been killed by a jealous mistress—and laughingly dismiss the claims of a primitive superstitious black boy (whom they had shipped back to Africa shortly after the crime) that he had killed his white messiah.

Wright was probably attempting here another allegory on the order of "The Man Who Lived Underground." The artist and his wife are representative of the white colonial mentality that regards natives as dolts who exist exclusively for the pleasures and convenience of their white masters. Babu, on the other hand, suggests mass African man, rootless, directionless, partially detribalized—existing somewhere between the Christianity of his rulers and the paganism of his ancestors—between the modern world and the primitive. He adores his white master as a god who represents for him all strength and wisdom, and

slaughters him in ritual fashion in hopes of assimilat-
ing that strength and wisdom. Possibly Wright is saying here that the white man had to kill his god—particularly those anti-worldly aspects of him—in order to
build so glitteringly a materialistic civilization—and
that Babu in murdering his white master god frees the
black man to build a similarly developed civilization.
But whatever the interpretation the allegory fails. The
dialogue is wooden, the characters too contrived, and
the plot, hovering somewhere between realism and
fantasy, is too fantastic or not fantastic enough.

"Big Black Good Man," which first appeared in
Esquire in 1957, is the last short story Wright published in his lifetime. Possibly it is the last he ever
wrote. In any event it represents a more traditional
approach to storytelling in that Wright here avoids
confining himself exclusively to dialogue. On the
other hand "Big Black Good Man" deviates from the
usual Wright short story. For one thing, the narrative,
by Wright's standards at least, is practically plotless.
Scarcely anything "happens." There is no violence,
practically no external narrative action, and no change
of milieu. The entire story is told in terms of the
emotions, attitudes and reactions of a white man, an
old night-porter who sits behind his desk at a cheap
waterfront hotel in Copenhagen. As the story opens,
he is discovered drowsily reminiscing about his youth
as a sailor when suddenly an enormous black seaman,
obviously American, enters and demands a room, a
bottle of whiskey, and a whore. Olaf is used to re-
quests like these and ordinarily does his best to com-
ply. He does not regard himself as prejudiced but feels
now an almost instinctive terror and hatred for this
black man who makes him feel so puny and white.
Although he wants to, he finds himself incapable of
refusing the Negro his demands—and, among other
things, provides him with Lena, a prostitute, for the
length of his stay. After six days the Negro prepares to
leave, but just prior to his departure he puts his massive hands around Olaf's neck. After he leaves, Olaf is

sure the black man wanted to humiliate him—to prove to Olaf how easy it would be to kill him. Consumed with hatred and shame, he fantasies the Negro's death at sea—he fancies he sees him drowning, about to be consumed by a white shark. A year later the Negro returns; Olaf cries out that there are no rooms, but the Negro replies that he does not intend to stay at the hotel this time. He thereupon presents Olaf with six shirts—one for each day he had spent with Lena the previous year—and informs him that he is going to live with Lena at her home. Olaf, in tears, confesses he feared that the Negro had intended to kill him when he measured his neck. The Negro, on his way out, laughs and calls back, "Daddy-O, drop dead!"

The story thus probes Olaf's psyche not simply in terms of his behavior, but mainly in terms of his dreams, fantasies, and memories. For the first time Wright has assumed the role of the enemy—and tells the story from his point of view. For all intents and purposes, Olaf is a normal petty bourgeois. He owns his own home, is fond of his wife and children, loves to putter about in his garden, and is not dissatisfied with his job. To be sure he is smug; there are no great depths to Olaf's passions. How then account for his sudden obsession, his terror? To Wright's credit, he does not attempt to explain, only to record. But the reader may gather insights nonetheless. Olaf's hatred is not socially conditioned; he is a Dane, and Danes are presumably relatively free of racial prejudice. Moreover, he has been a sailor and seen all parts of the world, and hence may be regarded as a cosmopolitan of sorts. Finally, it is probably true that Olaf has himself never consciously mistreated nor remembered feeling any animosity toward the other colored guests in the hotel. Are Olaf's reactions then instinctively racial? Do they suggest a repository of violent race memories buried beneath the placid exterior—of which Olaf was himself unaware?

Olaf's reactions are, of course, deep-seated sexual

responses, feelings of sexual inferiority—but, perhaps, above all, feelings of terror of the raw, intense sexuality of life that the Negro represents. Olaf sees the Negro as a "huge black thing that fills the door;" he has "snakelike fingers," a neck like a bull, a voice that "booms," and "wide and flaring nostrils." In describing him thus, there can be little doubt that Wright deliberately portrayed his black giant in romantic fashion—"His chest bulged like a barrel; his rocklike and humped shoulders hinted of mountain ridges; the stomach ballooned like a threatening stone." [16] There is then something regal, something suggestive of Prester John perhaps in this magnificent figure that strides across Olaf's soul from another world.

One now senses a new element of race pride in Wright's portrayal; the tone of proud defiance has somehow been stilled and replaced by a note of contained racial triumph. It is not quite racial revenge, but it is nonetheless interesting to note that Wright has now reversed the imagery of much of *Uncle Tom's Children*. Instead of white, there are now "black shadows," "black mountains," "black clouds like a stormy sky descending" [17] on the terrified Olaf. Yet despite the black sailor's mythic proportions Wright still manages to keep him down to earth, chiefly by means of dialogue. Somehow the Negro's "Daddy-O, drop dead!" suddenly transforms him to one more cynical, jazzy American. There is to be sure bitterness in the Negro's recognition that Olaf had been hating him all along—but in the midst of the bitterness there is the almost amused observation that such hatred can no longer harm him. It would of course be impossible to say whether Wright had intended "Big Black Good Man" to be the last word on what it means and feels to be a Negro. One can only say on the basis of this story that Wright himself came, momentarily at least, to a sense of pride and self-adjustment. Ironically, though, he could only do this by imagining what the white man felt.

6

Foreshadowings: *Lawd Today*

Lawd Today, Richard Wright's first novel (published
posthumously in 1963), is in some ways more sophisticated than his second, the more sensational *Native
Son*, which established his popularity, and to a large
extent his reputation. It is ironic that this should be so
in view of the fact that *Native Son* has subsequently
come to be regarded as a brilliant but erratic work by
an author who was perhaps ignorant of modern experimental techniques in prose fiction. For had *Lawd
Today* been published when Wright completed it,
such an impression might never have gained accept-
ance. If the novel reveals anything about its author, it
indicates that Wright had learned his Joyce, his Dos
Passos, his James T. Farrell, his Gertrude Stein only
too well. It is not that *Lawd Today* is a hodgepodge of
the styles of the above authors—actually, Wright is
usually in good control of his material—but that
Wright here appears as much interested in craftsman-
ship, form and technique, as he is in making explicit
social comment. Indeed, social comment derives from
the way Wright structures the novel—twenty-four
hours in the life of a Negro postal worker—and the
theme does not confine itself to Negro oppression but
says something about the very quality of life in urban
America. Moreover, Wright uses here for the first
time a Negro anti-hero: Jake Jackson is a loutish, heavy-
handed, narrow, frustrated, and prejudiced petit
bourgeois who, though unable to cope with his envi-

ronment, refuses to reject it—and is incapable of dreaming of a life different from the kind he knows. Yet, for all his limitations, Wright invests him with a sense of life that simmers just below the surface of his dreary existence. Here then lies the crux of Wright's success, for despite the huge indebtedness to other modern authors, the book is distinctly Wright's and the life and times he evokes are as immediate and as crushingly felt as his more popular radical fiction.

Wright was, of course, a Communist when he wrote the novel; he must have been a Party member for at least three years before *Lawd Today* was completed, but even a cursory glance at its contents will reveal what the Party would have found objectionable about its author. For one thing his principal character is a far cry from the ennobled oppressed proletariat that Communists liked to depict at this time. Jake is not only disagreeable; his sense of oppression stems principally from what Farrell has called "spiritual poverty" rather than from overt racial and social causes. In other words Wright portrays a soul already corrupted rather than a Negro struggling manfully to maintain his integrity against a hostile, threatening environment. It is of course implicit in the whole of *Lawd Today* that Jake's sickness is environmentally induced, that the environment is itself sick, immature, and devious, but there is scarcely ever any explicit reference to capitalist exploitation. Indeed, Jake himself has faith in the system. Secondly, although the story takes place some time in 1935 or 1936 in the Chicago Negro ghetto, only the most casual mention is made of Communism or Communists (Jake is a virulent "anti-Red"), despite the fact that there existed a considerable body of Communist organizational activity on the South Side at that period. (Wright himself may have been a Party organizer.) Needless to say none of Wright's Negroes undergoes any lightning conversion to socialism; as a matter of fact, they are all racists in their own way. Finally, Wright, in the course of the novel quotes from three "bourgeois" writers (Van Wyck Brooks, Waldo Frank, and T. S. Eliot), each of whom was a particular anathema to the recognized Party aesthetician, Michael Gold. There are then obvious reasons why Wright chose not to publish the novel at the time he wrote it. His relationship to the Party intelligentsia, already sensitive, would have been considerably exacerbated. Yet Wright's decision to keep the manuscript, despite his knowledge that the Party would have disapproved, arouses the suspicion that notwithstanding his dedication to the Party, somewhere in the back of his mind he foresaw the possibility of leaving the Party and using the story.

The novel is divided into three sections ("Commonplace," "Squirrel Cage," and "Rats' Alley"), each of which covers roughly eight hours in Jake Jackson's day. The first part, well over half the book, traces Jake's activities from the moment he awakens with a peculiarly disturbing dream in the morning until the time he goes to work in the afternoon. In the course of his day, Jake beats up his wife (whose demands on his income he feels are excessive), goes out into the neighborhood and loses at "policy numbers," loiters in front of a movie house regarding its rather flamboyant posters, gets a haircut, wanders aimlessly and restlessly about the city, plays cards for a while with his friends, resumes his wanderings, observes a Negro medicineman vending a "Cureall for All the Divers Ailments of the Human Body," and watches a Negro parade in which the participants wear uniforms of varying splendor representing the ranks, orders, and titles of a new, imaginary anticipated African empire. In sharp contrast to the transitory pomp and pride of this latter vision, Jake and his friends know that they must spend eight dreary, monotonous hours in the night shift of the Chicago main post office sorting letters. The second section of the novel, "Squirrel Cage," deals with this portion of Jake's day.

In "Squirrel Cage" Wright describes each of Jake's

duties at the post office in assiduous detail—as if, in order to understand Jake one must understand his work. And this indeed becomes true as part of the dull, heavy, perfunctory nature of his chores is somehow mysteriously transferred to his personality and outlook. Part of Jake's day is given over to obtaining an advance loan on his salary. To do this he must first prove to the personnel authorities that he is a provident husband and worthwhile risk. Jake discovers in the process that he is in real danger of losing his job since his wife has again gone to the postal authorities (she has apparently visited them several times in the past) complaining of his vicious treatment. Jack fortunately had anticipated this kind of trouble and had earlier arranged that a bribe be paid to a corrupt postal official in order that he be allowed to keep his job. Jake finally manages to borrow a hundred dollars from the paymaster, but only after he promises to pay usurious interest rates. He and his friends plan to celebrate Jake's good fortune at the end of their work shift.

"Rats' Alley," the third part of *Lawd Today*, takes Jake and his comrades into a lurid night spot frequented by Negro gangsters, hoodlums, and prostitutes. Jake lavishly offers to pay for all the food and entertainment his friends require. In the midst of what can only be described as a massive orgy of feasting, drinking, and dancing, Jake discovers his hundred dollars is gone. When he accuses his prostitute girl friend of helping a pickpocket steal his money, he is kicked and thrashed by the club patrons and thrown out into the subfreezing cold of the early February morning. Angered, humiliated and frustrated by this final twist of bad luck, Jake somehow manages to stagger home under the weight of all the liquor he has been drinking. When he sees his wife sleeping, he proceeds to beat her up unmercifully, and stops only when he falls to the floor asleep in a drunken stupor.

As a kind of choral accompaniment to all of Jake's

activities throughout the day, a radio blares forth from time to time the principal events in Lincoln's life. It is Lincoln's birthday, February 12, and the "glorious" career of the Great Emancipator serves as ironic contrast to the sordid enslavement of the bondsmen's progeny. For Wright makes it clear that despite Jake's legal freedom, he is indeed a slave. As Jake figures it, the next sixteen years of his life is mortgaged away in debt simply to pay for his wife's medical expenses (Jake had once persuaded her to have an abortion and the consequences to her health seem irreparable). But Jake has other debts as well. He owes money to neighborhood shopkeepers, particularly grocers. He must pay in graft to keep his job—and he owes now at the end of the novel the hundred dollars more that he borrowed in advance on his salary. Each time Jake tries to improve his situation, he discovers himself more and more deeply in debt. But if Jake is the hapless victim of a ruthless money system, he is even more a slave to the values of the civilization that exploits him. For Jake too strives for what Wright has called elsewhere the American "lust for trash." He dreams of the millionaire life he would have if he could win at the policy game. He implicitly accepts graft as a political way of life—and expresses no resentment that he must pay a bribe to keep his job. Indeed, he rather admires the people to whom he must pay his money. Although he is heavily in debt, Jake regards with pride and a sense of achievement the ten new suits he has bought that are hanging in his closet. He is apparently captivated by Hollywood notions of sex, heroism, and adventure as he earnestly studies the posters for a lurid Hollywood film in front of a movie theater. He envies gangsters because "they have a plenty of fun. Always got a flock of gals hanging on their arms. Dress swell in sporty clothes. Drive them long, sleek automobiles. And got money to throw away." [1] For Jake all women are "meat," to be conquered physically, but eschewed in any long term relationships. Jake also accepts un-

critically all the current Negro middle-class shibbo-
leths, pieties and prejudices of America in the face of
what he knows to be the truth. He believes million-
aires have their troubles just the same as ordinary
people do. He regards America as the freest, happiest
nation on earth and views as Reds people who criticize
his native land. Communists are "crazy"; they are
unable to run their own country and want to run
America. "Why don't they stay in their own country if
they don't like the good old U. S. A.?"[2] Jake agrees
with his barber that the "colored folk ought to stick
with the rich white folks" if they want to "get anywhere." Although Jake cannot tolerate his wife's long-
suffering, bleeding-heart Christianity, he believes one
has to take God seriously "because you can't do
nothing without 'Im." Finally, Jake shares in a characteristic touch of American xenophobia that "what's
wrong with this country [are] too many Jews, Dagoes,
Hunkies, and Mexicans. We colored people would be
much better off if they had kept them rascals out."

But besides being enthralled by some of the shod-
diest values of American civilization, Jake is as much
in bondage to subjective impulses, instincts and feelings which he only dimly understands. Perhaps the
principal difficulty lies in his inability to acknowledge
to himself the welter of contradictions he feels about
himself as a Negro. The central revelation of Jake's
nature is his dream which opens the novel. Jake
dreams he is hurrying up a long flight of stairs. He is
bending all his energy to reach the top, but try as he
may, he does not appear to be making any progress;
the steps seem endless. Unable to stop he hears the
voice of his boss urging him on, insisting that he come
at once, and Jake continues to run. The dream in a
sense relates not only the futility of Jake's strivings—it
is all he can do, apparently, to remain in the same
place—but announces the theme of the book—the
senselessness, the purposelessness, the absurdity of his
life. Nonetheless, all of Jake's energies are directed

towards denying the reality of his situation. In his way, of course, much of the time Jake is denying to himself that he is a Negro—since he knows in a profound sense that the goals he wants to achieve are denied him because he is a Negro. Jake will thus identify himself with white people in chauvinistically hating "foreigners" and "Reds." He will strive mightily before the mirror each morning to remove the kinks from his hair so that he will look less Negroid. He will try to overcompensate the shame of his blackness by buying expensive, ostentatious clothes he cannot afford. In denying his identity, he denies his experience as well. He seriously fancies he can resolve all his problems by winning at numbers and consults dreambooks for the lucky combination. He bitterly hates and resents his wife whom he regards as the source of all his difficulties when she is, after all, but another symptom of the malaise of being a Negro in America. Sometimes Jake and his friends will attempt to lose sight of themselves over games of cards, liquor, or women. Or on other occasions they will surrender themselves under the guise of good-natured camaraderie to an orgy of self-hatred and race deprecation by telling "nigger" jokes.

But this does not by any means tell the whole story about Jake. There are moments of bitter lucidity, resentment, and self-pity as when Jake and his companions discover a white postal worker eavesdropping on a conversation they have been having about women: "Yeah, a white bastard's always thinking we never talk about nothing but that." But there are moments too when Jake and his friends are capable of discovering vicarious revenge: "Lawd, it sure made me feel good all the way down in my guts when old Joe [Louis] socked Baer." What Wright does here is describe the slow dissolution of southern folk elements in the character of Jake and his friends as they face a new impersonal fragmentation of their lives in the city. Both Jake and his friends had migrated from the South to Chicago—to find better jobs, to look for freedom—but they have not yet quite forgotten their peasant orientation. They often speak of the South with bitterness. As they reminisce and compare their present condition to what they once experienced, they express a kind of folk humor or break into occasional "down home" rhyme:

'There ain't nothing worse'n a Southern white man but two Southern white men . . . .'
'. . . and the only thing worse'n two Southern white men is two Southern rattle snakes!'

. . . .

'Don't like a liver
Don't like hash
Rather be a nigger
Than poor white trash' [3]

But not all of their memories are so bitter. One of the attributes of Jake's southern nature is a kind of sensuous hedonism which undergoes an explosive transformation as a result of his city experiences. Just prior to the close of their work day, Jake and his friends remember the South in lush, physical terms. "You know we use' to break them honeysuckles off the stem and suck the sweetness out of 'em." The talk drifts to women and the men long to break out of their squirrel cage (which is what they call the post office) and find release from all the petty, meaningless activities of the past eight and a half hours. When the gong booms announcing the end of their shift, they are psychologically conditioned for the orgy that awaits them at the night club. All the accumulated frustrations that Jake has suffered throughout the day are now forgotten as he gives himself in joyous abandon to food, liquor, jazz, and women. It is as if all of Jake's secret memories, dreams, and desires have suddenly become accessible to him for only a short time —and he must bend all his energies to make them materialize. Jake expands with generosity and ebullient spirits, and wishes his friends to share in his good fortune. Even after he is thrown out of the club beaten, drunk, and cheated of his money, he is able to cry out in the February cold, "BUT WHEN I WAS FLYING I WAS A FLYING FOOL!" and "WHEN YOU GET TO WHERE YOU GOING TELL 'EM ABOUT ME!" It is only in these episodes where Jake loses himself in baccanalian revelry that he becomes somehow oddly attractive. Sunk below the dull, heavy, platitudinous exterior there boils a zest for life which can find expression only in frenzied moments like these. But even here the moment passes too rapidly and Jake descends to the depravity of wife-beating.

Lawd Today is thus as much an indictment of the northern and southern cultures that produced Jake as it is of Jake himself. Jake's naïveté, his credulousness, his superstitious nature are all made to appear southern traits that Jake carried North with him—but they are traits that northerners use to exploit him. Jake and his fellows are constantly being besieged by purveyors of dreambooks and quack health-cures for everything from arthritis to alcoholism and sexual impotence. Jake, in turn, has apparently adapted himself to the deviousness and deceit of which he has been made such a victim. In his own way Jake is a petty corrupter and cheat—conspiring with an abortionist to deceive his wife that a baby would be detrimental to her health, paying bribes to keep his job, scheming calculated lies in order to obtain illegal loans. Thus, wedded to Jake's naïve ignorance is a furtive duplicity—which allows him to survive.

In producing *Lawd Today* Wright had clearly worked from several prose models. The Studs Lonigan trilogy by Wright's fellow Chicagoan comes immediately to mind. Jake, like Studs, was incapable of transcending the limitations of his environment; both protagonists as a result suffer an impoverishment of the spirit, though both in different circumstances possess conceivably heroic possibilities. Their activities, strivings, ambitions are shown to be petty, meaningless, and futile—matching somehow the shallowness of their characters, the dreariness of their culture. Above all, both Wright and Farrell aim at achieving a phonographic reality of the speech patterns in their principal protagonists, their conversational colloquies, and their silent musings. Wright takes great pains to record Jake and his friends rendering stale jokes, and iterating platitudinous remarks about life, religion, and politics. Often the things they say do not correspond to what they really think or feel—but they are unaware of any inconsistency or hypocrisy on their part. Their conversations do, nonetheless, have the effect of conveying the dehumanization of their lives as they exchange perfunctory, hollow banalities.

Wright's desire to achieve as close a verisimilitude as possible to the conditions and quality of Jake's environment extends to reproducing verbatim the words on billboards, movie marquees, newspaper headlines, the words of popular songs, "throwaways," and advertising leaflets advising Negroes new "guaranteed" ways of discovering their lucky numbers, God, and various other desirable goals. Crudely written and vulgarly conceived this material would be almost laughable were it not for the fact that the reader knows it is intended to exploit the very anxieties and insecurities it promises to assuage. Perhaps Wright's tour de force—along the lines of total recall and reproduction—is a recreation of a bridge game Jake plays with his friends. Each card held by each player and each play he makes is carefully described. Finally, as in his early short stories, Wright attempts not only to reproduce accurately the words people speak, but the volume and sounds they make as well. Here for example are the opening remarks of a street corner medicine man as he prepares to vend his mystery elixir:

> "LAdees 'n' Gen'meeeeeeens: Ah 'm 's the SNAKE MAN! Ah wuz BO'N 'bout FORTEEEEY YE ars erGO on the banks of the FAMOUS NILE in the great COUNtreeeeeey of AFRIker, yo' COUNtreeeeeee 'n' mah COUNtreeeeeey—in

tha' LAN' where, in the YEARS gone by, yo' FATHER 'n'
mah FATHER ruled SUPREME!" [4]

On occasion Wright moves away from the phono-
graphic-photographic renderings of Dreiser and Farrell
and experiments with a kind of poetic-journalese
stream of consciousness that owes something perhaps
to Dos Passos, such as when Jake scrutinizes the posters of a Hollywood adventure film:

> The first poster showed a bluehelmeted aviator in a
> bloodred monoplane darting shooting speeding zoom-
> ing careening out of a bank of snow-white clouds in
> hot pursuit of two green monoplanes . . . and at the
> side of the hero sat a golden-haired blue-eyed girl oper-
> ating a machinegun spewing fire and death and the
> girl's hair was blown straight back in the wind and her
> eyes were widened in fear and
> the next poster showed the hero creeping into
> a darkened garage on feet of feathers upon a small rat-
> like creature who had a huge hammer.[5]

In certain other respects Wright tried to probe even
beyond consciousness and suggest the instinctive psychic forces that determine Jake's behavior. The theme
of the novel is announced implicitly in Jake's stair-
climbing dream. But besides Jake's dreams (and daydreams) Wright discloses glimpses of Jake's inner
nature in circumscribed, repetitive phrases and expressions he catches in fragments and snatches of Jake's
conversation. (Wright probably derived the idea from
Gertrude Stein whose "Melanctha" was one of his
favorite stories.)

Unlike many "proletarian" writers of the thirties,
Wright was not afraid to use metaphor or imagery
when he believed the occasion demanded. The unadorned statement of fact, the flat, prosaic rhythms of
speech characterize a large proportion of the novel,
but as we have seen, not all. Besides occasional forays
into streams of consciousness and unconsciousness,
Wright, from time to time, lyrically evokes character

and mood—("outside an icy wind swept around the corner of the building, whining and moaning like an idiot in a deep black pit")—sometimes even, humor. In the beginning of the novel as Wright describes Jake at his toilet, Jake's head becomes a battlefield, the unruly strands of hair, "wire entanglements of an alien army" and Jake's comb, the patriotic army bent on destroying the invaders.

> The battle waxed furious. The comb suffered heavy losses, and fell back slowly. One by one teeth snapped until they littered bathmat and washbowl. Mangled and broken things they lay there, brave soldiers fallen in action, many of them clutched in the death grip of enemy hairs.[6]

There are moments of course when Wright, the new novelist, loses control of his narrative. The action, for the most part, unfolds from the point of view of Jake, but Wright intrudes on two occasions, assuming the role of the omniscient author, in order to explain how the "numbers" racket works, and what the various technical procedures in the post office signify. Admittedly these are both rather specialized areas, but a more practiced writer would have known how to introduce them without jarring the focus of the reader. Wright, too, is sometimes clumsy at handling transitions: at times one feels that Wright wants to reveal Jake's views on religion, or race, or politics, and that these topics are rather forced out of Jake instead of flowing from the natural sequence of events or Jake's thoughts.

But these are minor details in what is otherwise an interesting, ambitious, and lively novel. Wright in the main succeeded in what he set out to do. He wanted to evoke the sights, the sounds, the smells of Jake's Chicago. He wanted to reveal its paucity of spirit, its shallowness of character, its false morality, its sanctimonious pride, and the energy and violence of life that exists below its dreary, placid exterior. All these are reflected in Jake's psychology and exemplified in one way or another in his activities of the day. In this respect, of course, Wright must have been inspired by Joyce's *Ulysses*. There is danger in drawing too strong an analogy between the two books, but there are some related elements. Jake is obviously no Leopold Bloom, but the movements of the two anti-heroes are traced over a twenty-four hour period; moreover, both Joyce and Wright fix on a particular date (June 16, 1904 and February 12, 1936) in order to render the lives of their protagonists, and the specific tangible "feel" of their cities, more believable. Jake's twenty-four hour cycle does not assume the mythic proportions of Leopold's—but perhaps that is the point. Jake's life is meaningless on any terms. Indeed, at one other point, the two men are poles apart. Leopold's great sadness stems from the loss of his son, whereas one of the sources of Jake's misery is that he did not want his child and deceived his wife into aborting it. The wives of both men have drifted from their husbands, one dreaming solace in fantasies of other lovers and romance, the other dreaming peace in illusions of a Christian afterlife. Finally, both men seek relief in orgiastic revelry—Bloom in Night-town, and Jake at the Calumet night club—only to return to a continuing cycle of experience to which they are both bound.

Superficially, *Lawd Today* does not appear to have much in common with Wright's later fiction of flight, violence, and oppression. But a closer look will reveal that many of the themes for which Wright would become famous are present—if only in muted form. The Negro, as villain-hero, which so shocked the Negro community at the time of publication of *Native Son* was evidently first described by Wright several years earlier in his unpublished novel. Negro nationalism, and perhaps even Wright's dreams of Africa, are embodied in Jake's fantasies. *"Lawd if I had my way, I'd tear this building down!"*

He saw millions of black soldiers marching in black armies; he saw a black battleship flying a black flag;

he himself was standing on the deck of that black battleship surrounded by black generals; he heard a voice commanding: "FIRE!" Booooooom! A black shell screamed through black smoke and he saw the white head of the Statue of Liberty topple, explode and tumble into the Atlantic Ocean.[7]

Not unconnected with themes of Negro and African nationalism are problems relating to the huge twentieth century Negro migration from the rural South to the highly industrialized areas of the Midwest and Northeast. It was only under conditions peculiar to city life that nationalist activities and minority movements flourished. This is an idea Wright would develop at length in *12 Million Black Voices* and in his "Introduction" to Cayton and Drake's *Black Metropolis*. In *Lawd Today*, Wright shows in part the rapid erosion of the Negro's folk ties and his gradual assumption of a new mode of life. Finally, the futility of Jake's strivings in the face of a hostile environment, his Sisyphus-like failure to reach the top of the stairs as illustrated in his dream, are translated easily into the absurdity of the existentialist hero. Wright must have made this latter observation himself after he broke with the Communist Party. He took the original manuscript of *Lawd Today* with him to Europe and rewrote it in several parts. The result was the existentialist *Outsider*, published in 1953–some seventeen years later.

7

Revolution: *Native Son*

Whatever may be said of the aesthetic value of *Native Son*, its impact is as resounding now as it was in 1940 when the novel was first published. This, in spite of the fact that its flaws are more obvious today than they could have been in the last years of the Depression when proletarian literature still enjoyed a vogue. Nearly all the weaknesses and embarrassments that we have come to recognize in proletarian fiction are present in *Native Son*, yet somehow the reader is not so conscious of them. One reason is that Wright's protagonist, unlike the usual array of proletarian victims, is thoroughly the anti-hero. He is not simply weak like Dreiser's Clyde Griffiths (one of Wright's chief influences here is *An American Tragedy*), but he is an outright coward. Indeed the first section of *Native Son* is called "Fear" and traces all the different kinds of fear that determine Bigger Thomas's actions. He is incapable of warmth, love, or loyalty; he is a sullen bully—and he enjoys his first sense of humanity and freedom only after he commits two murders.

Still in certain other respects *Native Son* possesses many of the characteristic failings of proletarian literature. First, the novel is transparently propagandistic—arguing for a humane, socialist society where such crimes as Bigger committed could not conceivably take place. Secondly, Wright builds up rather extensive documentation to prove that Bigger's actions, behavior, values, attitudes, and fate have already been determined by his status and place in American life. Bigger's immediate Negro environment is depicted as being unrelentingly bleak and vacuous—while the white world that stands just beyond his reach remains cruelly indifferent or hostile to his needs. Thirdly, with the possible exception of Bigger, none of the characters is portrayed in any depth—and most of them are depicted as representative "types" of the social class to which they belong. Fourthly, despite his brutally conditioned psychology, there are moments in the novel when Bigger, like the heroes of other proletarian fiction, appears to be on the verge of responding to the stereotyped Communist version of black and white workers marching together in the sunlight of fraternal friendship. Finally, Wright succumbs too often to the occupational disease of proletarian authors by hammering home sociological points in didactic expository prose when they could just as clearly be understood in terms of the organic development of the novel.

Yet if *Native Son* may be said to illustrate some of the more flagrant conventions of proletarian fiction, there are aspects of this novel that reveal Wright exploring problems of character portrayal, prose style, and theme. As has already been suggested, there is first of all the sympathetic presentation of perhaps one of the most disagreeable characters in fiction. That Wright had to a large degree achieved this may be attested to as much by the loud protests of his critics as by the plaudits of his admirers. Second, although *Native Son* makes its obvious sociological points, one should bear in mind that for well over two thirds of the novel Wright dwells on the peculiar states of mind of his protagonist, Bigger, which exist somehow outside the realm of social classes or racial issues. Indeed Wright himself frequently makes the point that Bigger hangs psychologically suspended in "a shadowy region, a No Man's Land, the ground that separated the white world from the black that he stood upon." [1]

Hence if categorizing terms are to be used, *Native Son* is as much a psychological novel as it is sociological, with Wright dwelling on various intensities of shame, fear, and hate. A third problem is that of style. Since the point of view throughout the novel is that of the illiterate and inarticulate Bigger, Wright had to discover a means of communicating the thoughts and feelings Bigger is unable to express. At times Wright frankly interprets them for his readers, but on other occasions he reveals them in terse sentence rhythms, in objectified images of Bigger's environment—the way the streets look to him, the feel of the sleet and the snow against his skin, the sounds of a rat rustling in the darkness of a vacated tenement—and in dispassionate, unadorned accounts of Bigger's movements which in themselves are accurate conveyors of Bigger's emotions.

To require of his readers that they identify themselves with the violent emotions and behavior of an illiterate Negro boy is no mean feat—but Wright's success goes beyond the shock of reader recognition with its subsequent implications of shared guilt and social responsibility. A rereading of Wright's novel some twenty-five odd years after its publication suggests that Wright was probing larger issues than racial injustice and social inequality. He was asking questions regarding the ultimate nature of man. What indeed are man's responsibilities in a world devoid of meaning and purpose? That Wright couched these questions in what one critic has described as the linguistics of Marxism has perhaps deterred readers from re-examining *Native Son* in the light of its existentialist implications. The reader may properly ask: was not Wright himself somewhat deluded as to the efficacy of his Communist frame of reference? The answer must be to a certain extent, yes. But a further question then suggests itself. Since moral responsibility involves choice, how can Wright's deterministic Marxism be reconciled with the freedom of action that choice implies? The contradiction is never resolved, and it is precisely for this reason that the novel fails to fulfill itself. For the plot, the structure, even the portrayal of Bigger himself are often at odds with Wright's official determinism—but when on occasion the novel transcends its Marxist and proletarian limitations the reading becomes magnificent.

The plot has a kind of classic simplicity dividing itself into three "books" within the novel. The time span represented in the first two books is a little less than seventy-two hours. The third book covers perhaps a little more than a month. Book I, "Fear," traces a day in the life of twenty year old Bigger Thomas from the time he wakes up in the morning and kills a rat in the squalid one room tenement apartment he shares with his mother, sister, and brother —to the time he creeps back into bed twenty-one hours later having just murdered a white girl. Bigger's day has thus symbolically begun and ended in death. But Wright proceeds in this first book to document Bigger's activities in such a way as to prove that all of Bigger's waking existence is a kind of meaninglessness —a kind of death. After killing the rat Bigger goes out into the streets where he loiters with members of his gang and plots (fearfully) to rob a white man's store. Later he goes to a movie and sits through a banal Hollywood doublebill. Wright shows here how, although these films lack substance, the glitter of the great white world beyond titillates Bigger and, at the same time, frustrates him all the more. When Bigger returns from the movie, he has a savage fight in a pool room with one of the coconspirators in the proposed robbery. Bigger next goes off to a job interview that had been arranged for him by the relief authorities. Mr. Dalton, Bigger's prospective employer, is a rich white man philanthropically inclined toward Negroes. (He also, the reader discovers, owns considerable real estate on Chicago's South Side and has a controlling interest in the house in which Bigger's family lives.)

He hires Bigger as a chauffeur and Bigger's first assign-
ment is to drive the Daltons' daughter, Mary, to the
University the same evening. Once in the car Mary
redirects Bigger to drive her to another address where
she is joined by her lover, Jan. Mary and Jan are
Communists and want to befriend Bigger; they sit up
front with him in the car and ask him all sorts of
intimate questions, but Bigger reacts with suspicion
and fear. It is women like Mary, he reasons, who have
made things hard for Negroes. They make Bigger take
them to a Negro restaurant where they embarass him
by forcing him to join them at a table. Afterwards
Bigger drives them around the park while Mary and
Jan drink from a bottle and make love in the back
seat. When Jan leaves, Bigger discovers Mary is much
too drunk to walk to the house by herself—and so he
carries her into her bedroom and places her on the
bed. He finds himself somewhat sexually stimulated,
but, just at that moment, Mrs. Dalton, Mary's blind
mother, enters the room. She calls to her daughter,
and Bigger, fearing what Mrs. Dalton will think,
places a pillow over Mary's head so that she cannot
respond. After Mrs. Dalton leaves, Bigger discovers
that he has accidentally smothered Mary to death. He
throws the corpse into a trunk and takes the trunk
downstairs to the cellar where he thrusts Mary's body
into the furnace. Then he carries the trunk out to the
car, since Mary had told him earlier she wanted him to
take it to the railroad station the following morning.
Thus ends Bigger's day—he goes home.

The entire action described in Book I totals fewer
than seventy-seven pages. Bigger's character and circumstances are related in a few quick almost impressionistic episodes—but the real plot movement does
not actually commence until Bigger confronts the
Daltons. Yet Wright has forecast Bigger's doom from
the very start. Bigger knows deep in his heart that he is
destined to bear endless days of dreary poverty, abject
humiliation, and tormenting frustration, for this is

what being a Negro means. Yet should he admit these things to himself, he may well commit an act of unconscionable violence. "He knew that the moment he allowed what his life meant to enter fully into his consciousness, he would either kill himself or someone else." And he knows as well that he will not always be able to delude himself. He tells his friend, Gus, early in the novel, "Sometimes I feel like something awful's going to happen to me." Hence, Bigger's principal fear is self-knowledge—and this, of course, is the theme and title of Book I. The other kinds of fear that constitute Bigger's life are by-products of this basic terror.

All Bigger's actions stem from his fear. Bigger hates whites because he fears them. He knows they are responsible for his immobility, his frustration, yet he is unable to admit even his fear. Were he to do so he would be admitting simultaneously a profound self-hatred. He thus rechannels his hatred and aggressions towards other Negroes—and thereby, momentarily at least, assuages his ego. He is afraid, for example, to steal from a white storekeeper and he is terrified that his friends can read his heart—so he attacks them in order to prove to himself his courage. He hates Mary Dalton who, he fears, will jeopardize his job, and he regards all her overtures as efforts to humiliate him. He kills her because he fears the help he has given her will be misunderstood. Bigger's nature then is composed of dread and hate. He hates what he fears—and his bravado and violence are merely compensatory illusions of his terror.

The second book, "Flight," describes Bigger's awakening sense of life at a time, paradoxically, that his life is most in danger. Although his killing of Mary was an accident, Bigger decides that he must assume full responsibility for her death. Hence, for once in his life he will know the consequences of an action he has "voluntarily" taken. In killing Mary, he feels, he has destroyed symbolically all the oppressive forces that have made his life a misery. Thus perhaps her death was not so accidental as it seemed at the time. Bigger enjoys a sense of potency, of power and freedom that he has never before experienced. He knows something, has done something that the whites do not know, and proceeds now to act with new found self-esteem. Ironically, the self-esteem takes the form of performing more dastardly acts compounding his crime. He plans to lay the blame for Mary's disappearance on Jan. Jan was, after all, the last white person who had seen Mary alive; he was a Communist—and Bigger knew most Communists were hated. Bigger succeeds in implying Jan's guilt and Jan is arrested and held for questioning. Meanwhile Bigger has revealed to his girl, Bessie, that he is somehow implicated in Mary's disappearance—it is now front page news—and Bessie reluctantly agrees to help Bigger to extort ransom money from the Daltons under the pretense that their daughter has been kidnapped. Bigger's plan falls through when reporters discover Mary's charred bones in the furnace—and Bigger is forced to flee. He finds Bessie and together they conceal themselves in a flat of an unused, vacated tenement. Bigger realizes that Bessie is at best an unenthusiastic coconspirator and so he decides he must kill her or she will some day reveal his whereabouts to the police. He makes love to her and after she has gone to sleep he smashes her head in with a brick. The monstrousness of this second murder exhilarates Bigger all the more. He has freely exercised his will—something he had never been able to do before. Now he has the chance to "live out the consequences of his actions." Bigger for the first time was "living truly and deeply no matter what others might think." [2]

Thus Bigger has opted the identity of a murderer. In an absurd, hostile world that denies his humanity and dichotimizes his personality, Bigger has made a choice that has integrated his being; "never had he felt [such] a sense of wholeness." [3] Ironically, Bigger has assumed the definition the white world has thrust upon the Negro in order to justify his oppression. If the Negro is a beast at heart who must be caged in order to protect the purity of the white race, Bigger will gladly accept the definition. It is at least an identity—preferable to that of someone obsequious, passive, and happily acquiescent to his exploitation. Bigger's choices are moral and metaphysical—not political or racial. He might have chosen love or submission; instead he has elected violence and death as a sign of his being, and by rebelling against established authority—despite the impossibility of success—he acquires a measure of freedom. None of the above is intended to deny that oppressive environmental factors do not limit the modes of Bigger's actions; nonetheless, environment by itself does not explain Bigger. So far as the reader can determine, Bigger's original alienation from the Negro community was made of his own free choice. His mother, his sister, his girl—each has made an individual adjustment of some sort to the conditions of Negro life, but Bigger cannot abide by either his mother's religiosity, his sister's Y.W.C.A. virtue, or Bessie's whiskey—all seem to him evasions of reality. Yet Bigger's rejection of Negro life was only a negative choice; his acts of murder are positive—thereby to a degree humanizing—since he is quite prepared to accept the consequences.

The remainder of Book II represents some of Wright's best prose—perhaps for sheer excitement the best narration Wright would ever produce. The sentences—spare of adverbs and adjectives—possess a taut, tense rhythm corresponding in their way to the quickening pace of flight and pursuit as the police inexorably draw in on Bigger. Bigger flies from one street to the next, from one tenement to the next; he is chased across roofs until finally he is flung down from the chimney to which he has been clinging by the pressure of the water directed at him from the hoses of firemen.

Book III, "Fate," attempts to draw together all the

significant strands of Bigger's life. Like Dreiser in *An American Tragedy*, Wright here tries to show how all of society has become involved in Bigger's crimes—indeed how all society, white and black, has a stake in Bigger's crimes. The newspapers, the police, and politicians use Bigger's capture and imprisonment as instruments for their own self-aggrandizement. The Communists defend him although it is made clear that even they do not altogether understand him. Futile attempts are made to convert him to Christianity. Philanthropists and the business community are even implicated in Bigger's crimes inasmuch as both are exploiters of the Negro. Racists burn crosses in various parts of the city—and outside the courtroom in which Bigger is being tried a howling white mob cries for Bigger's blood. Max, Bigger's attorney, in a useless but eloquent address to the jury tries to explain Bigger's crimes in terms of the devastating psychological blows of Negro history (slavery) and social and economic exploitation.

Immediately after his capture Bigger assumes a pose of sullen apathy. But Max's genuine efforts to help him have awakened in Bigger a vague sense of hope and trust in men. Max, Bigger knows, is the only person who has ever really cared to find out about him. Bigger needs Max and looks forward to his visits. He knows that the jury will doom him, but this does not disturb him so much. Throughout the agony of his trial, Bigger has been trying to puzzle through the meaning of his life and world. He has always lived so isolated from other human beings that he is no longer sure. He asks Max, but even Max, whom he likes, can only respond in historical and socio-economic terms. Conceivably, some day, Max tells him, men will be able to express their beings in terms other than struggle and exploitation. But, although moved, Bigger cannot ultimately accept this. The essence of life is violence and power. "But, what I killed for, I am!" [4] What he killed for must have been good since he hadn't really known he was alive until he killed. Bigger elects to face death on the same principles that had made his life meaningful.

The chief philosophical weakness of *Native Son* is not that Bigger does not surrender his freedom to Max's determinism, or that Bigger's Zarathustrian principles do not jibe with Max's socialist visions; it is that Wright himself does not seem to be able to make up his mind. There is an inconsistency of tone in the novel–particularly in Book III, "Fate," where the reader feels that Wright, although intellectually committed to Max's views, is more emotionally akin to Bigger's. Somehow Bigger's impassioned hatred comes across more vividly than Max's eloquent reasoning. Indeed the very length of Max's plea (sixteen pages in the Harper edition) suggests that Wright, through Max, protests perhaps too much–that he is endeavoring to convince himself.

The whole of Book III seems out of key with the first two-thirds of the novel. Where Books I and II confine themselves to a realistic account of Bigger's thoughts and actions, Book III tries to interpret these in a number of rather dubious symbolic sequences. Early in "Fate," for example, Wright describes a somewhat improbable scene in Bigger's cell, where Bigger is made to confront all the people with whom he had previously been involved: there are the Daltons, Jan, a Negro preacher, his mother, brother, and sister, three members of his street gang, Max, and the district attorney. Everything is highly contrived–as if Wright is placing before Bigger's eyes all the major influences that have made up his life. In another scene of transparent "symbolism," Bigger, after a rather trying day in court, flings the wooden crucifix that the preacher had given him out of the cell door, thereby signifying his rejection of Christian options. Perhaps the most flagrant violation of verisimilitude is Max's plea to the jury. Although Max undoubtedly makes good sociological sense and possibly even a sound assessment of Bigger's character, his defense is not the sort that would ordinarily persuade a jury. A more realistic approach to the intensely hysterical court-room atmosphere Wright describes would have been for Max to plead Bigger guilty of some sort of insanity —rather than to suggest that Bigger is a helpless victim of American civilization. Finally, Book III contains a number of improbable colloquies between Bigger and Max. Here Bigger is almost unbelievable. After twenty years of conditioning to mistrust every human being, especially whites, he suddenly opens up and bares his soul to Max. The point Wright is making is a good one: that no one has ever before cared to understand Bigger as a human being—and not as a symbol; no one has ever before granted him his dignity. (Max does not even understand this until the very end.) None-theless, to suggest that Bigger would respond so quickly to Max under such straitened circumstances is to make excessive demands on the credulousness of the reader.

The failures of *Native Son* do not then reside in the proletarian or naturalistic framework in which Wright chose to compose his novel. Any great artist can after all transcend the limitations of form—if he so wishes. In any event if Wright had stuck closer to an organic naturalistic development, his novel might have achieved more consistent artistic results. The basic problems of *Native Son* lie elsewhere. There is an inconsistency of ideologies, an irresolution of philo-sophical attitudes which prevent Bigger and the other characters from developing properly, which adulter-ate the structure of the novel, and which occasionally cloud up an otherwise lucid prose style. There are three kinds of revolutionism in *Native Son*—and none of them altogether engages the reader as representing Wright's point of view. Max's Communism is of course what Wright presumes his novel is expressing— yet this kind of revolutionism is, as we have seen, more imposed from without than an integral element of

Bigger's being. The artificial structure of Book III, for example, is written around Max's Marxist defense of Bigger. Sometimes Bigger is himself visited by visions of a Communist utopia—but these are so out of character that even Wright cannot long sustain him in these attitudes. On these occasions Bigger dreams a kind of sentimentalized racial brotherhood clothed in a rhetoric and vocabulary utterly beyond his experience. When Bigger is feeling kindly towards his Communist friends, the metaphors become embarrassing: "The breath of warm hope which Jan and Max had blown so softly upon him turned to frost under Buckley's [the district attorney] cold gaze."

A second kind of revolutionism is of a Negro nationalist variety—and this is far more in keeping with Bigger's character. Part of the reason Bigger accepts responsibility for the death of Mary is that he realizes he hates all whites with such an intensity that it gives him extreme pleasure to think that he had killed her deliberately. He enjoys, moreover, a new sense of potency, a power over whites, since he is now in possession of knowledge of which whites are ignorant. His is a reverse racism. As Max puts it:

> Every time he comes in contact with us, he kills! . . . Every movement of his body is an unconscious protest. Every desire, every dream, no matter how intimate or personal, is a plot or a conspiracy. Every hope is a plan for insurrection. Every glance of the eye is a threat. *His very existence is a crime against the state!* [5]

Sometimes Bigger's nationalism takes more of a political form: "There were rare moments when a feeling and longing for solidarity with other black people would take hold of him. He would dream of making a stand against that white force. . . . He felt that some day there would be a black man who would whip the black people into a tight band and together they would act." [6]

But Bigger's nationalism, whatever its components, is nothing compared to what Camus has subsequently described as metaphysical revolution. "Human rebellion ends in metaphysical revolution," Camus writes in *The Rebel*—and it is in the role of the metaphysical revolutionary that Bigger looms most significantly for modern readers. The metaphysical revolutionary challenges the very conditions of being—the needless suffering, the absurd contrast between his inborn sense of justice and the amorality and injustice of the external world. He tries to bring the external world more in accord with his sense of justice, but if this fails he will attempt to match in himself the injustice or chaos of the external world. In either case the principle is the same: "He attacks a shattered world in order to demand unity from it." Bigger's is a "shattered world." In *How Bigger Was Born* (1940), Wright describes it as a "world whose fundamental assumptions could no longer be taken for granted . . . whose metaphysical meanings had vanished." By rejecting such a world and by identifying himself with the world of violence and strife he knows to be true, Bigger has given his life meaning and clarity. He thus becomes like the romantic criminal, Satan, who as Camus describes him, acts as he does because since

> violence is at the root of all creation, deliberate violence shall be its answer. The fact that there is an excess of despair adds to the causes of despair and brings rebellion to that state of indignant frustration which follows the long experience of injustice and where the distinction between good and evil finally disappears.[7]

Bigger's crimes then signify something beyond their therapeutic value. In a world without God, without rules, without order, purpose, or meaning, each man becomes his own god and creates his own world in order to exist. Bigger acts violently in order to exist and it is perhaps this fact, rather than his continued undying hatred of whites, that so terrifies Max at the close of the novel. It is possible that Max senses that as a Communist he too has worked hard to dispense with the old social order—but the metaphysical vacuum that has been created does not necessarily lead men like Bigger to Communism, but may just as easily lead to the most murderous kind of nihilism. Max's horror was to become Wright's dilemma two years after the publication of *Native Son* when Wright himself would leave the Party. Wright could no longer accept the assumptions of Communism any more than he could those of racist America. Yet the prospects of a new world of positive meaning and value seemed very distant indeed.

It is then in the roles of a Negro nationalist revolutionary and a metaphysical rebel that Wright most successfully portrays Bigger. And it is from these aspects of Bigger's character rather than from any Marxist interpretation that Wright's sociology really emerges. For the metaphor that Wright uses best to illustrate the relationship between the races is "blindness"—and blindness is one result of Bigger's racist nationalist pride. Prior to his conversion by murder Bigger has blinded himself to the realities of Negro life as well as to the humanity of whites. As in *Uncle Tom's Children*, he vaguely discerns the white enemy as "white tides," "white blurs," "icy white walls," and "looming white mountains." He is therefore unable to accept Jan's offer of friendship, because he blindly regards all whites as symbols of oppression. It is only after his metaphysical rebellion has been effected by the death of the two girls that Bigger acquires sight. When he looks at his family, he sees them now as blind as he had been; he understands what it means to be a Negro. Buddy, his brother "was blind . . . Buddy, too, went round and round in a groove and did not see things. Buddy's clothes hung loosely compared with the way Jan's hung. Buddy seemed aimless, lost, with no sharp or hard edges, like a chubby puppy . . . he saw in Buddy a certain stillness, an isolation, meaning-lessness." When he looks at his mother he sees "how soft and shapeless she was. . . . She moved about slowly, touching objects with her fingers as she passed them, using them for support. . . . There was in her heart, it seemed, a heavy and delicately balanced bur-den whose weight she did not want to assume by disturbing it one whit." His sister, Vera "seemed to be shrinking from life in every gesture she made. The very manner in which she sat showed a fear so deep as to be an organic part of her."

Bigger's new vision enables him to see how whites see him as well—or more precisely, how blind whites are to his humanity, his existence. Whites prefer to think of Negroes in easily stereotyped images—in im-ages of brute beast or happy minstrel. They are incapa-ble of viewing black men as possessing sensitivity and intelligence. And it is this blindness that Bigger counts on as the means of getting away with his crimes. When he schemes with Bessie to collect ransom money from the Daltons, he tells her the (white) police would never suspect them because they "think niggers is too scared." And even well-meaning people like Mr. and Mrs. Dalton are blind to the sufferings of Negroes. Believing that acts of charity can somehow miraculously banish in Negroes feelings of shame, fear, and suspicion, the Daltons lavish millions of dol-lars on Negro colleges and welfare organizations—while at the same time they continue to support a rigid caste system that is responsible for the Negroes' degradation in the first place. Mrs. Dalton's blindness is symbolic of the blindness of the white liberal phil-anthropic community. Additionally, the Communists, Mary, Jan, and Max, are just as blind to the humanity of Negroes as the others—even though they presuma-bly want to enlist Negroes as equals in their own cause. For Mary and Jan, Bigger is an abstraction—a symbol of exploitation rather than someone whose feelings they have ever really tried to understand. Although he does not know it, this is really the reason Bigger hates them. Even when Mary concedes her blindness, she has no idea how condescending she sounds to Bigger. "Never in my life have I been inside of a Negro home, yet they must live like we live. They're human." [8]

In the final analysis *Native Son* stands on shifting artistic grounds. Had Wright managed to affix a different ending more in accord with the character of Bigger and the philosophical viewpoint he seeks to embody, the novel might have emerged a minor masterpiece. Yet, for all its faults, *Native Son* retains surprising power. The reasons are still not clearly understood by even present-day critics. It is not simply that what has been called the Negro problem has once more intruded itself into the national consciousness, if not the national conscience—although "sociology" should certainly not be discounted as an important factor. Nor is it merely the sensational nature of the crimes Bigger committed, compounded as they were with racial and sexual overtones. In part, of course, it is the terrible excitement, the excruciating suspense of flight and pursuit that Wright invests in his best prose. In part, too, it is the shock of unembellished hatred in Wright's portrayal of a seemingly nondescript apathetic Negro boy. James Baldwin writing of *Native Son* says every Negro carries about within him a Bigger Thomas—but that the characterization by itself is unfair in that there are complexities, depths to the Negro psychology and life that Wright has left unexplored. To depict Bigger exclusively in terms of unsullied rage and hatred is to do the Negro a disservice. In Baldwin's view Bigger is a "monster." This, of course, is precisely the point Wright wishes to make—and herein lies its most terrible truth for the reader. Wright is obviously not describing the "representative" Negro—although he makes clear that what has happened to Bigger can more easily befall Negroes than whites. He is describing a person so alienated from traditional values, restraints, and civilized modes of behavior, that he feels free to construct his own ethics—that for him an act of murder is an act of creation. But can such a person exist? Yes, if his actual experiences contradict the interpretations civilization ordinarily puts on human action. Although Bigger dreams the American dreams, he knows he can never realize them because he is a Negro. If the civilization rejects him out of hand, he will reject the traditional and acceptable means and values for achieving the rewards that civilization has to offer. This is not a conscious rationalizing process on the part of Bigger— it is almost second nature. How else can he do more than survive? But do such "monsters" as Baldwin calls them exist? Our tabloids could not exist without them. But even supposing they do not commit murder, their sense of isolation and alienation is growing in the face of an increasingly impersonal, industrialized mass society. And in mass, the isolated, the alienated, are capable of consent or indifference to nuclear holocaust or extermination camps. It is perhaps in this respect that *Native Son* is so much more disturbing a novel today than when it was first published. It is not that Bigger Thomas is so different from us; it is that he is so much like us.

order in his own personality—and despairs, as the novel closes, that such a reconciliation can ever be effected in society as well. *The Outsider*, then, is Wright's most pessimistic novel in that he poses problems that he states frankly fail of solution; it is a novel in which the reader finds Wright endeavoring nonetheless to work these problems out—hoping, evidently, that in the course of his exploration he would discover the form of his novel. But because his "ideas" fail him, the very structure of the novel fails him at the end—and *The Outsider* can at best be described as a very imperfect work of art.

Wright, of course, had always conceived of the novel as a means of working out his ideas. "Writing," he told William Gardner Smith in 1953, "would always be a way of thinking aloud over issues—posing the problems and the questions as to their solution—posing them only, not answering them." [3] The chief problem he poses in *The Outsider* is how to achieve individual freedom without impinging on the freedom or humanity of others. It is this central problem on which all the other problems of the novel hinge. They fail to resolve themselves because Wright attaches a set of conditions to his notions of freedom which make the attainment of freedom an impossibility. Freedom fails because man is so hedged in by predetermined psychological molds that he cannot act rationally or calculatedly. He is instead a creature and prey of physical and emotional compulsions over which he has no control. Every man, Cross discovers, is invested with a sense of dread and terror (perhaps connected with the birth trauma), with a sense of guilt (inherited from a civilization that tries to impose curbs on his violent amoral nature, his lust for power, his desire to become a little god), with a sense of injustice (the world seems to promise so much and offers all too frequently only meaningless suffering and death), and with the sense, however remote and unacceptable, that the universe is purposeless, that God does not exist, and that human life is insignificant. Cross, in endeavoring to seek his freedom, finds himself capable of shedding all illusions regarding the true nature of "civilization," "morality," Christian "values," and human motivation; they are all in the final analysis man's inventions to conceal from himself the fierce libidinal impulses of his own nature and the senseless chaos of the world in which he exists. But Cross is incapable of coping with his own physical needs, with his pride, with his self-love and self-hate, and his inborn sense of justice. In maintaining these attributes, Cross fails as god and remains human and, ironically, unfree.

Wright structures Cross's odyssey for freedom into five books. The first book, "Dread," is largely expository. It relates the dilemma of Cross Damon, a twenty-six-year-old postal clerk whose wife, pregnant mistress, and mother are making all sorts of financial, moral, and emotional demands upon him. (It will be recalled that Wright's then unpublished *Lawd Today* served as a working model for *The Outsider*.) Cross, in his daily dealings with the three women and his fellow postal workers feels something akin to nausea. His social and legal obligations have enslaved him. He has inherited from his mother a sense of guilt and foreboding regarding his relationship to women and his general awareness of amoral physical and sexual longings. Yet he is aloof and intellectual enough to know that the dread he experiences is psychological (i.e., it stems from his religious upbringing, the demands of his women, and the knowledge that he lives in a world devoid of reason, God, or universal values). Wright stresses here that Cross's views have been arrived at as a result of his reading and his individual relationships—and only secondarily because he is a Negro. Allusion is made early in this first book that because Cross no longer believes in God, he becomes his own god and acts accordingly in somewhat symbolic fashion. One of Cross's friends describing Cross's

first years in the post office recalls that Cross, con-
vulsed with laughter, would throw money down on
the street from the eleventh floor and watch the com-
motion of "little ant-like folks . . . scrambling and
scratching and crawling" after the coins. And after the
money was gone, they would look up at the window,
their mouths open like "little fishes out of water," and
Cross would say when they looked like that, they were
praying.

One evening after having engineered an eight hundred dollar loan from the post office, Cross discovers
himself trapped in a freak subway accident. He manages to extricate himself but finds that he has left his
overcoat behind. Later he learns that another Negro
who had been riding on the same car was killed and
had been identified as Cross Damon since Cross's overcoat was found lying next to his smashed body.
Cross suddenly realizes that inasmuch as everyone
thinks him dead, he can begin life anew with no obligations. He hides for a while in a brothel-hotel to
make sure that no one suspects he is still alive, and
there, ironically, discovers a fellow postal worker who
had attended his funeral. Cross suddenly turns on
him, knocks him unconscious, and flings him out of an
eleventh story window. The following day Cross
boards a train for New York, relieved somewhat of the
dread that had pursued him all his life.

Cross moves from dread to "Dream," the title of
Book Two. Wright indicates Cross is now "dream"
because presumably having no identity, he is unable to
relate to persons and things around him. In a sense he
possesses no reality but observes passively:

> As silent as a mirror is believed
> Realities plunge in silence by.[4]

Not until Cross obtains a past and a social role,
Wright hints, will he become a man again. On the
train Cross meets two persons, each of whom will
figure strongly in his life afterwards. The first is Bob

Hunter, a dining car waiter, who inadvertently spills coffee on a white woman customer. The woman screams that the Negro had deliberately scalded her and threatens to report him. Hunter turns to Cross to testify for him but Cross can only give him a false name and address. The second person Cross meets is Ely Houston, a hunchback New York district attorney. The two men engage in long philosophical disquisitions—not unlike Raskolnikoff and Porfiry—about crime and the ethical criminal. Both agree that there are a growing number of men and women who are finding it impossible to accept traditional Christian values. Finding themselves increasingly alienated and isolated by a mass urban industrial society, they tend to take the law into their own hands—indeed feel they have the *right* to break the law. They differ from the ordinary criminal in that the latter expects and wants to be captured; the ordinary criminal posits an orderly, coherent world against which he rebels—the ethical criminal regards the world as chaotic and meaningless. Houston and Cross both agree as well that the Negro in America is in a better position to perceive the realities of existence than the ordinary white man, inasmuch as the Negro, though Westernized, is excluded from full participation by virtue of his color. Cross intuits that Houston is just as much the criminal as any of the prey he pursues. He protects himself from his amoral criminal impulses by cynically assuming the cloak of the policeman. Yet Houston is as much an Outsider as Cross—he recognizes that society and civilization are mere sham—disguises to protect men from the knowledge of their own bestiality. Houston, in his turn, is very favorably impressed by Cross's intellect and insight. He is especially struck by a remark that Cross makes: "Man is nothing in particular." [5]

When Cross reaches New York, he manages, after considerable effort and much ingenuity, to appropriate the name and identity of a Negro, Lionel Lane, who had just recently died. Later he meets Bob Hunter on the street who informs him that the railroad had fired him because of the incident on the dining car. Cross learns Bob is a Communist and through Bob is introduced to two white Communists, Gil and Eva Blount. Cross is perversely fascinated by Gil's almost instinctive desire to wield power over him. He recognizes in Gil the atrophying of all human and subjective feeling. Gil is a cynical man who uses and manipulates men's dreams in order to control and rule them. Gil and other Communists like him are in their own way as criminal as Cross and Houston. As Book Two closes, Cross accepts Gil's invitation to live with him and Eva in their Greenwich Village home in order, ostensibly, to provoke the Blounts' fascist, Negro-hating landlord. Cross secretly anticipates with joy the struggle he is about to have with Gil and his fascist enemy over the possession of Cross's criminal soul.

It is in Book Two that Wright's novel first really begins to go awry. Book One is almost exclusively narrative; the characters are feasible and behave according to their own inner laws. Even Cross's dilemma, grim as it is, and his own subsequent efforts to extricate himself, are understandable if not altogether praiseworthy. Cross's character and situation—the alienated, aloof, and contemptuous Negro intellectual, mired in a slough of depressing, sordid, near-hopeless circumstances—is a subject worthy of a fine novel. Where did Wright go wrong? One can begin to sense it toward the close of Book One. Cross's murder of the postal worker, Joe, in the brothel, is at once comprehensible and yet at the same time bewildering. Cross feared that Joe would betray him and thereby reinvolve him in a morass of responsibilities and accusations even worse than the ones he had known before the accident. Yet, after performing the deed, Cross seems strangely unmoved by the horror of his actions. It is somehow hard to believe that a man who has been engulfed by dread and fear all his life can all at once reject his wife and children, his pregnant mistress, his mother—and commit a brutal murder—and yet move about apparently untroubled by qualms of conscience. It is possible but hardly probable. This suggests one of the main problems with *The Outsider*. Although Wright has attempted to create in Cross a creature who earnestly endeavors to discipline his emotions, and act only according to his intellect and perceptions, he remains nonetheless, Wright tells us, a creature of impulse and desires. Yet his most significant and violent actions are determined almost always by his intellect—and he thereby becomes something other than human.

Book Two centers itself almost exclusively around Cross's intellectual motivations. Again Wright portrays Cross here as being utterly devoid of guilt. Whatever dramatic, violent, or significant actions he has taken in the past concern him only as analytical problems, seldom as issues in which his whole consciousness has been and still is involved. But if Cross's central passions are now almost exclusively intellectual, so, astoundingly, are those of the persons he is destined to meet. Indeed, so focused are they on certain intellectual or philosophical positions, that they too seem scarcely human. Ely Houston, for example, exists solely to elicit Cross's views on life. Their fortuitous meeting on the train is hardly convincing—and even less convincing is the philosophical exchange that they undertake which is couched in a strange melange of sociological and existential jargon. More to the point, however, is that Houston and Cross do not really seem to have a dialectic at all. Indeed, since they both share identical viewpoints, there is not any of that intellectual excitement that obtains, for example, in a Shaw play. If Houston represented traditional morality, or occupied, say, a Catholic theological position, there might exist some justification for the colloquy. As the text stands, Wright could just as easily have placed Cross's words in Houston's mouth and vice versa. Similarly, it is clear as Book Two ends that

Gil Blount, the Communist, is another intellectual, philosophical robot—whom Cross will hate precisely because they think so much alike.

Book Three is called "Descent" because here Cross, having presumably acquired an identity and anchored himself in some kind of social relationship to the Communist Party, is now free to plumb the depths of his nature and act according to his own laws. He realizes that the Communists only want to use him, and he himself looks forward to using them. Indeed, bad faith is a rule of life. All of his life he had practiced bad faith in his individual relationships. Moreover, he realizes that "the daily stifling of one's sense of terror . . . the far-flung conspiracy of pretending that life was tending toward a goal of redemption, the reasonless assumption that one's dreams and desires are realizable—all of these hourly, human feelings were bad faith." [6] Cross goes to live with the Blounts in their apartment. He recognizes at once that Eva is a frightened, fragile creature who is obviously not at ease in the situation. He surreptitiously reads Eva's diary and discovers that Gil had deceived her by marrying her for political reasons. Eva had been a well-known artist, and the Party had obviously gained prestige by her marrying a Communist. Gil's betrayal of Eva confirms Cross's suspicions that the Party is concerned exclusively with power, that its strength lies in its distribution and codification of power—and that humanitarian and economic motifs are merely a facade to a grim Orwellian truth. Indeed the rewards of Party membership really lay in the satisfaction individuals derive in wielding absolute power over persons of lower Party rank. The price of absolute power however lies in the abject surrender of freedom to one's Party superior. The Party cynically recognizes the human need to play the role of a god and uses this insight to gain control over men. "Here was something more recondite than mere political strategy; it was *life* strategy using political methods as its tools." [7] Cross is, of course, thrilled and outraged at the Communists' cynical exploitation of men's dreams and anxieties. He is determined at least to preserve his freedom and humanity. Cross's test is not long in coming. Herndon, the Negro-hating landlord, who lives on the floor below the Blounts, warns Cross to leave. Cross informs Gil, who decides to visit Herndon the same evening. A terrific struggle ensues in which the fascist and the Communist batter away at one another with all their strength. Cross enters ostensibly to stop the fight—but seizes the opportunity to kill them both. He then flees upstairs to Eva, to whom he pretends he has been unsuccessful in obtaining entry to Herndon's apartment. Cross believes at the time that he killed Gil and Herndon that he was destroying "gods" who would enslave him—but realizes afterwards that in killing them he has set himself up as a little god in their stead.

Thus the stage has been set for Book Four which Wright aptly names "Despair." For Cross despairs that in acting freely as he did, he became himself—he realized his true nature, the nature of all men, violent and murderous. In destroying the monsters that would deprive him of his humanity, he has become a monster himself. Book Four therefore is essentially an elaboration of the despair that dawns on Cross at the close of the preceding book. The police arrive and come reluctantly to the conclusion that Blount and Herndon had killed each other. Cross again meets his old friend, Ely Houston, and Houston rejects the idea that a third person could have committed the murders since he would have had to be someone for whom Western values and traditions had no meaning. Such a person would be hard to imagine, Houston says. Cross, meanwhile, is having a love affair with Eva, but realizes that her love for him is based on a complete misunderstanding of his character. She imagines him a victim like herself, and takes almost a maternal interest in him. Cross, on the other hand, wants to protect her from betrayers and deceivers like himself. His despair is compounded. He discovers, too, that Hilton, a high ranking Communist, has secret information that Cross killed Blount. Cross goes to Hilton's hotel room and shoots him—but not before they have a lengthy colloquy on the nature of man, life, and politics. Hilton, just before he dies, remarks improbably that there are no values or meaning: "Sweep your illusions aside. Get down to what is left and that is: life, life, bare naked unjustifiable life; just life existing there and for no reason and no end." [8]

After Hilton's death Cross becomes once more suspect, not only by the police, but by the Communists themselves, who are far shrewder. At one juncture he is again interrogated by another high-ranking Communist, Blimin, who asks Cross who he really is and what his views are. Cross's response—fourteen pages—is almost as long as Max's defense in *Native Son*. In effect Cross expresses a philosophy of history not unlike the one Wright propounded in his very important essay in Cayton and Drake's *Black Metropolis*. Civilization and its institutions, its laws, its rituals are the mythology men create to conceal from themselves the bleakness of the human heart. Science, industry and urban living have rendered men immune to the mythology of traditional relationships and values. Mankind—or at least a good portion of it—is returning to the pre-Christian stage of development where every man becomes a law unto himself in a universe that is governed by no laws. Communism and fascism are merely the political expression of twentieth century atheism —the organization of power structures as absolute by modern standards as religion once had been in pre-industrial days. Cross tells Blimin that he has no intention of opposing the Communist doctrine, but he believes that if the Communists were really serious about their humanitarian protestations, they would fight the capitalists on other than ideological or economic grounds. Wright, through Cross, reveals here his real concern with the quality of American life. The mass of Americans, he says, are deluded and enthralled by a cheap and mindless materialism. "The only real enemies of [the] system . . . are those outsiders who are conscious of what is happening and seek to change the consciousness of [those] . . . being controlled." [9] Cross's speech is certainly not the kind that would endear him to the Communists—and since he knows that his life is in danger, the reader might regard him as being unnecessarily reckless. But the fact of the matter is that by this time Wright's narrative is so out of hand that the reader is almost past caring. The murders Cross has committed are incredible—not only from the point of view of what Wright asks his readers to regard as Cross's motives (they are all matters of compulsion; Cross's victims "offend him"), but also from the point of view of execution. The inability of the New York police to solve these crimes suggests that Wright must have regarded law enforcement officers as somewhat less than cretinous. Perhaps the principal trouble, however, lies in Wright's portrayal of Cross. In determining he would create an intellectual monster who rejects Western values, Wright had no place to take him other than along the path of more murders. (Indeed at one point Cross even contemplates murdering Eva.) How someone who has so successfully purged himself of "feelings" as Cross can suddenly fall in love is of course another matter. One is left sadly to conclude that even Wright did not understand his main protagonist. The compulsions Cross succumbs to are not the mere murderous intellectual whims of a god who would crush an insect that annoys him, but instead deep-seated, suppressed drives of malice against persons who would use him to satisfy their own psychic needs and deny him his own personality in the process.

From infancy on, Wright tells us, Cross was at the mercy of a mother who imparted guilt and dread into his soul to such a degree that Cross constantly trembled at the brink of his amoral nature—which he thought he knew. But perhaps what he did not know was that the fear, trembling, and nausea that he felt are the suppressed and savage hatred of a mother who made him the scapegoat for all her sorrows. The demands made upon him by the other women in his life in the Chicago phase of his existence, which Wright relates in excruciating detail, have also made of him an unwilling instrument of their suffering. Hence Cross's anger at being used is understandable. When Cross murders two Communists and a fascist, his motives seem to derive more from what he regards as his victims' desire to enslave him psychologically, rather than from any detached, intellectualized, conscienceless "compulsion" on his part. What the Communists and fascist would do to Cross if they had him in their power is precisely what his mother, wife, and mistress had already done to him. In a sense, Cross murders his women when he crushes his enemies.

Although Wright stresses that Cross's philosophy and attitudes have been arrived at as a result of his individual experiences and thinking, and not because he is a Negro, there can be little doubt that racial resentments figure in Cross's psychology. It would be unfair to state that they constitute a major motivation, yet to discount them glibly would be to do the character of Cross—indeed the character of the novel —an injustice. If, as is made clear from the very beginning, Cross is his mother's son, then it must be remembered too that Cross's mother is a product of Mississippi racism and southern Negro piety. The dread she invests in Cross's soul is the dread she learned as a Mississippi Negro. From time to time an inverse race hatred (Negro for white) manifests itself throughout the novel. Gladys, Cross's wife, declares she loathes working with whites and relates how, when she was a child, she saw her mother savagely mistreated by a white man. Working-class Negroes in a bar make a joke to the effect that whites are terrified that people in flying saucers may be colored. Cross must pretend to be an abject "darky" in order to acquire a birth certificate. Bob Hunter's wife says she does not go to church because she could never kneel before a white man. And the Communists attempt to seduce Cross by their promises of racial revenge. If race were not an important element in Cross's character and environment, why would Wright take the trouble to relate all these instances of racism?

Book Five, "Decision," carries the novel to its unlikely conclusion. Cross is apprehended once more by the police and is made to confront Ely Houston again. Houston tells him he has investigated his background and has discovered his true identity. He also tells him he has deduced Cross to be the murderer; his evidence is only psychological, but he is convinced that only someone of Cross's intellectual and philosophical orientation could have committed these crimes. Cross neither confirms nor denies his guilt. He then tells Cross that his mother has died. Cross remains unmoved. Houston is astonished at the indifference and heartlessness of his suspect. (Note the resemblance here to Meursault's indifference to his mother's death in Camus' *L'Etranger*.) Next Houston brings into the room Cross's wife and three boys. Cross still refuses to acknowledge them. Houston is astounded— but tells Cross to go; he knows he would not be able to persuade a jury of Cross's guilt, but is himself convinced that a man who feels no longer emotionally bound by Western institutions such as religion or the family is capable of committing any crime. He informs Cross before he leaves that the Communists suspect him as well and have been badgering the police to arrest him and charge him with murder. Cross returns to Harlem where he has been living with Eva and discovers that the Communists have been trying to convince her too that he is the murderer of her husband. Cross decides to make a clean breast of his guilt to Eva in the hope that in their reciprocal love

and trust he can build life anew. His decision (hence
the title of Book Five) proves fatal. Eva is so appalled at what she learns that she commits suicide.
There is another colloquy between Cross and Houston
and then Cross moves out into the streets of Harlem
alone. He notices he is being followed and he is convinced that the Communists are determined to kill
him. He hides for a while in a movie house but later
they catch up with him in the dark of night and shoot
him. Just prior to his death he whispers to Houston,
"Don't think I'm so odd and strange. . . . I'm not.
. . . I'm legion. . . . I've lived alone, but I'm
everywhere." [10] A new period is approaching, he warns,
in which men will no longer delude themselves about
their murderous nature and the meaninglessness of
existence. When Houston asks him what his life was
like, he answers that it was horrible because "in my
heart . . . I'm . . . I felt . . . I'm *innocent*. . . .
That's what made the horror."

Wright could obviously do nothing more with
Cross. The "logic" of his life committed him to increasingly hideous crimes until he himself would be
murdered. Cross, of course, admits his failure; he has
stripped himself of all illusions and discovers ultimately only his compulsions, his desires. And these
enslaved him. But as Houston puts it, desire is itself an
illusion because it is almost certain one never gets
what he desires. For man ultimately desires to be a
god (power); he wants everything.

Camus no doubt influenced Wright's conception of
Cross. Indeed some of Cross's expressions—"jealous
rebels," "ethical criminals"—appear to be taken verbatim from Camus' essays. More specifically, Meursault
in Camus' *L'Etranger* resembles Cross in ways that
Wright never acknowledges. Both men kill without
passion; both men appear unmoved by the death of
their mothers; both men apparently are intended to
represent the moral and emotional failure of the age.
Yet Meursault's psychology seems genuinely to derive

from the alienation and tedium of his life, while Cross's motivations are shrouded in Wright's own private socio-existentialist mythology. One of the most persistent myths about *The Outsider* is that since the Negro stands outside American life, he is better able to judge American values and American culture. Cross, for example, is somehow supposed to possess an objectivity and a detachment of which few white people are capable. Wright himself knew better. Practically all his works prior to *The Outsider* express the idea that continuing social and economic discrimination creates personality distortions in Negroes that often render them incapable of perceiving reality. To aver otherwise as Wright does in *The Outsider* is not being altogether honest.

But difficulties of this sort again suggest one of the major difficulties with so much of Wright's work, and that is that Wright will use materials that his artistic instincts must tell him are untrue—in order to make certain facts correspond to a particular intellectual or philosophical position that he may be espousing. In a sense this is what happens in his treatment of the Communist Party. However misguided, amoral, skeptical, or clever American Communist officials may have been, it is highly dubious that they were ever as utterly amoral or sadistically murderous as Wright makes them out to be. But for Wright's peculiar point of view he had to create Communists who spoke and acted like existentialist criminals. And presumably, because they are so spiritually alike, the Communists and the New York district attorney's office are capable of working together in pursuing the identity of Cross. Indeed the Communists put heavy pressure on Houston to arrest Cross for murder. That the New York district attorney's office would at all cooperate with Communists, let alone allow itself to be badgered by them, at the beginning of what has been called the McCarthy period (the novel takes place in 1951) is almost laughable. Yet this is the kind of disbelief Wright asks his reader to suspend.

The Outsider is a novel in which "ideas" dominate plot, character, even prose style. Indeed, the plot exists, as we have seen, as a kind of working out of Cross's philosophy of life. The characters frequently appear simply as representatives of intellectualized attitudes, or "types" borrowed from other works of fiction. Eva, for example, is a wooden figure so pure, blonde, and innocent, that she could stand in as the older sister of her prototype in *Uncle Tom's Cabin*. Houston, on the other hand, reminds one of the cunning intellectual and psychological Porfiry of *Crime and Punishment*. The name Cross Damon (Demon?) is itself a symbol of inverted Christianity and suggests any number of metaphysical rebels in Russian, French, and German literature. Indeed Cross's progenitor in American letters may conceivably be Melville's Captain Ahab. If Wright had been aware that his characters were so "symbolic" he might well have decided to place them in another kind of fictional form. What happens in *The Outsider* is that Wright has created allegorical figures whom he has described in a naturalistic context. The resulting confusion accounts for the failure of the novel.

If *The Outsider* is to be regarded as a part of Wright's spiritual autobiography, it will be remembered as representing the nadir of his pessimism. All of his works up to this point have concerned themselves with the pursuit and discovery of individual freedom. In *The Outsider* Wright is saying that freedom is an impossibility; that man will ever be a prey to his compulsions; that in seeking his freedom man becomes an enslaver of others. But along with the pessimism there exists the germ of hope. In rejecting Communism years before Wright had very nearly despaired of mass social action as a means of discovering freedom. Nonetheless his interests and activities in nationalist movements are evidence that Wright had not given up altogether. Still, he insisted as he had insisted earlier in his novella of 1944, *The Man Who Lived Underground*, that man must first know himself—

know the dark and mysterious proportions of his nature. Freedom without self-knowledge is a logical contradiction. Just before he dies Cross whispers to Houston the following:

> I wish I could ask men to meet themselves. . . . We're different from what we seem. . . . Maybe worse, maybe better. . . . But certainly different.[11]

In August, 1955, Richard Wright sent off a lengthy letter to his friend, the editor, Edward Aswell, in which he set forth his future literary plans. He intended to compose a trilogy of novels (the first of which had already been written, *Savage Holiday*) whose basic theme would be a celebration of life. Each of his books would be introduced by an extended prose poem describing the progress of a kind of life-spirit from the tiniest of one-celled organisms to the birth and death of a planet. Nothing came of the project, and it is doubtful whether Wright had conceived of such a grand scheme when he first began work on *Savage Holiday* two years before. Nonetheless his comments to Aswell are valuable inasmuch as they provide insights into Wright's point of view regarding his work. He was, he told Aswell, preoccupied with the individual and his society; "men need society," he wrote, "yet too much society kills them, nullifies their humanity."

The moral and psychological pressures that society imposes on men are the central issue of *Savage Holiday* (1954). In a sense the novel is but another presentation of the problem of *The Outsider*. In what respects is an individual morally obligated to uphold social values in a society that treats him shabbily—that denies him identity? Why is freedom so crushingly oppressive? Is freedom at all possible? If an individual is ridden by unconscious drives, wherein does his guilt lie? The fable Wright constructs around these questions suggests that he had come no closer to their resolution than when he wrote *The Outsider*. Yet the

narrative is itself somewhat more plausible, the characters a bit more credible, and—perhaps because he did
not strive so hard to make his existentialist points—the
theme emerges more clearly. Still, for all that, *Savage
Holiday* falls far short of genuine artistic achievement,
possibly because of a kind of textbook quality to the
story it tells. The novel is divided into three parts, the
title of each beginning with the same letter, "A." It is
as if there exists an inexorable flow of consequences
stemming from the first letter of the first word of the
titles of "books" or "parts" in Wright's novels. The
alliterative titles imply a kind of determinism which
hint from the start the futility of the pursuit of freedom. Yet freedom is the central quest in all Wright's
fiction.

Part One is called "Anxiety" and traces the activities of forty-three-year-old Erskine Fowler, a white
"retired" insurance executive, during a summer week-
end. The novel opens with a Saturday night testimo-
nial dinner and ball given in honor of Fowler who has
presumably resigned his position after having given
thirty years service to Longevity Life (he had begun
working when he was only thirteen). A series of flash-
backs reveals that Fowler in actuality is being forced
out to make way for a younger man. Despite his
protestations he has been bullied, threatened, and humiliated by the higher echelon of company executives
into pretending that he is voluntarily resigning. He
leaves the festivities early and returns to his small,
immaculate bachelor apartment on the tenth floor in
the East Seventies. The next morning he is awakened
by Tony Blake, a five year old neighbor boy, beating a
toy drum on the balcony that fronts his apartment.
The balcony is apparently accessible to anyone living
on the tenth floor since its entrance is to be found in
the public hallway outside his apartment. Later that
morning, just before he is about to take a shower,
Fowler steps momentarily out of his apartment,
naked, to pick up his Sunday newspaper. The door

unexpectedly blows shut and he discovers himself locked out. Fowler, whom Wright had been describing as a paragon of almost stuffy middle-class virtue and respectability, becomes suddenly terrified and ashamed. Like a trapped animal he runs back and forth along the corridor, covering himself as best he can with his newspaper. He climbs into the self-operating elevator to descend to the basement in order to get the superintendent's help, but the elevator is constantly being pulled up or down by persons on other floors who are waiting to use it. After several harrowing moments of redirecting the elevator to avoid being seen, Fowler manages to return to the tenth floor, still naked but as yet unnoticed. It suddenly occurs to him that he can probably hoist himself up through his bathroom window from the outside balcony. He dashes out onto the balcony and there discovers five year old Tony sitting astride his electric hobbyhorse. The child is so astonished at seeing a huge hairy naked man plunging toward him that he tumbles off his toy against the railing. The railing gives way and the child drops ten flights to the street below. Fowler jumps atop the hobby horse and climbs in through his bathroom window. He wonders now how responsible he is for the child's death. Should he inform the police what really happened? Or would they regard it simply as an accident? Was it not really an accident? Fowler surely did not expect to find the child on the balcony —and certainly he wished him no harm. What good would it then do to bring sensational publicity and attention upon himself? Was not the child's widowed mother really to blame? She was known to neglect Tony most days and in the evenings she was never home.

The first part of this novel, as in so many of his other books, contains some of Wright's best prose. Wright is always most effective in describing a character caught up in the dread and tension of flight—the terror and suspense of being discovered. The sentences, stripped of needless verbiage, become stark and severe—the rhythms clipped and taut. Fowler, in flight from all the fanciful demons that would expose him, reminds one in his way of the children of Uncle Tom who flee from the savagery of the racist South, or even Native Son in his desperate attempt to escape the police. And although the consequences of Fowler being discovered are far less threatening, the psychological terrors for him are immense, as his actions make clear. All the more pity then that Wright has to intrude from time to time to "explain" Fowler's behavior.

For *Savage Holiday*, in far too obvious a way, is a psychological novel. Not only are Wright's psychoanalytical interpolations a bit too condescending, but the character of Fowler is designed almost embarrassingly on a Freudian pattern. For example, in Part One Fowler compulsively touches the tips of pointed pencils in his inside breast pocket—and then later dreams that he is watching a man hack away at a V-shaped hollow of a tree in a forest. And to make certain that the reader does not miss the significance of the forest, Wright describes Fowler naked. "He stripped off his pajamas and loomed naked, his chest covered with a matting of black hair, his genitals all but obscured by a dark forest." [12]

Part One is called "Anxiety" because anxiety is intended to describe Fowler's psychic state at the opening of the novel. Nonetheless, it sounds no different from the nameless dread both Bigger Thomas and Cross Damon experience in Wright's two previous novels:

> He was plagued by a jittery premonition that some monstrous and hoary recollection, teasing him and putting his teeth on edge because it was strange and yet somehow familiar, was about to break disastrously into his consciousness. [13]

In part Fowler's anxiety stems from his new outsider vision. Like Cross Damon, Fowler, by virtue of his retirement, is freed from petty obligations and respon-

sibilities. He is now perforce compelled to confront
the yawning dread, the fearful unconscious impulses
that have haunted his soul since childhood. It is thus a
"hated freedom," an endless holiday in which freedom
is his imprisonment. He can no longer escape himself.
He is "trapped in freedom" and his anxieties are exacerbated by his inordinate terror at being discovered—
symptomatic, obviously, of something more profoundly disturbing in his nature. Then in endeavoring
to assess his guilt in the death of the child, Fowler is
made even more anxious. Finally, he worries that he
may have been seen on the balcony with Tony and
that someone may have reported him to the police.

Fowler's anxieties are an oddly bitter, ironic twist of
the original fact that he had once been an insurance
executive and knew as a successful investigator that
"insurance was life itself; insurance was human nature
in the raw trying to hide itself; insurance was instinctively and intuitively knowing that man was essentially a venal, deluded, and greedy animal." [14] Yet
knowing this Fowler had no insurance that his lot or
condition would be different from that of the rest of
the human race. Indeed, his being forced into "retirement" is the greatest joke on the concept of insurance
—particularly since Fowler had felt so young and secure at the time. Longevity Life, the firm for which
Fowler works, belies its name in its treatment of
Fowler. And the delusory life of the workaday world
must now give way to the terrible life of the human
unconscious.

"Ambush," the title of the second part of Wright's
novel, refers to the way long repressed, socially unacceptable thoughts and emotions come suddenly to the
fore to redirect human behavior. Still troubled by his
role in the child's death, Fowler goes to church and
becomes happily inspired by the thought that he has
acted somehow as God's agent. Tony's death, Fowler
tells himself, was divine retribution for his mother's
"loose" and immoral life. Fowler must in some fash-

ion redeem Tony's death by redeeming his mother—
bringing her to the ways of God. Returning from
church after having preached a brief sermon, Fowler
remembers Tony telling him how he had observed his
mother making love with several men, and how frightened he had been. Tony knew babies were conceived
in this fashion but believed that men and women were
fighting. Tony had lived in constant terror of violence
—a violence which he feared he would have to commit
himself when he grew to be an adult. Fowler could be
sympathetic with Tony because *his* mother had been
loose and promiscuous as well. Now it occurred to him
why Tony had been so frightened on the balcony
earlier that morning. He thought Fowler was one of
those huge naked hairy men he had seen with his
mother, and he feared Fowler would fight him too.

When Fowler returns home, he is told by the superintendent's wife, Mrs. Westerman, that Tony's
mother claimed she had seen on the balcony that
morning a pair of naked feet dangling in the air.
Fowler is almost sick with fear, but Mrs. Westerman
assures him that Mrs. Blake had had a lover staying
with her that morning and that she had probably been
drunk. Fowler determines to meet Mrs. Blake, but
before he can do so, the telephone rings. The first time
he answers his caller hangs up. On the second occasion, a thin reedy voice says to him, "I've seen everything," and then clicks the receiver down. When
Fowler does get to meet Mrs. Blake, he is caught in a
welter of feelings and his will is paralyzed. Was she his
secret caller—and could she be an informant? She
seems so helpless and forlorn, and in spite of himself
he is sexually attracted to her. He wants to protect and
help her. Possibly he could save her. He offers to help
in the funeral arrangements and she gratefully accepts.
Yet, later when he sees her again, he is puzzled, bewil-
dered, and angered by the frequent telephone calls
from men that she continues to get, and the tolerant
way she receives them. He fiercely accuses her of cal-

lousness and neglect, and when she responds in kind to his officiousness, he abjectly surrenders and tells her that he loves her. But when he returns to his own apartment and hears her telephone ring again through his wall, he is once more tormented by jealousy and anger.

There are moments of suspense and terror in "Ambush" that are the equal of anything Wright had written. Wright is especially good in conveying Fowler's dawning horror that some unknown person had seen and recognized him on the balcony with Tony. The telephone will now become Fowler's principal instrument of torture—first as the agent of a possible blackmailer, and second as the means by which Mrs. Blake communicates with other men. But despite passages of high narrative skill, the plot becomes contrived in order, one feels, to reveal Freudian insights. It is just too much coincidence that Tony should have the same kind of promiscuous mother that Fowler had had in his youth. And of course now one knows immediately that Fowler will react to Mrs. Blake in the same fashion he had once reacted to his own mother. In any event his feelings toward her will be identical to those repressed feelings he has had about his own mother. And now the reader knows too that Fowler's anxiety and dread have always centered around those buried feelings about his mother. And what these feelings are and always have been becomes more and more obvious as well. Fowler is both immensely attracted and loving—and intensely jealous and hating. He has apparently a tremendous need to play the role of the strong father, the protector and the supporter of the meek, passive, and submissive woman—but if that woman should assert her own identity, her freedom, her own independent personality, she awakens cold, murderous feelings in Fowler's heart.

The portraiture of Mrs. Blake at this point in the novel is elusive and vague—but this is not necessarily a weakness since she is described from Fowler's understandably distorted point of view. When Wright does allow her to speak, she sounds natural enough and behaves consistently, one feels, according to her own values. Perhaps the principal thematic weakness of Part Two lies in omission. In concentrating on Fowler's unconscious (there are even more psychoanalytical interpolations and explanations than in Part One) Wright seems to have quite forgotten the issue of Fowler's moral responsibility in Tony's death. It is not that psychology and morality are two separate and distinct issues—but that Wright, for some reason, really fails to connect them. Moreover, there was a suggestion in Part One that Fowler could have saved Tony from falling had he reacted sooner. Did Fowler unconsciously want Tony to die to save himself embarrassment later? Did Fowler, who had been unconsciously identifying himself with Tony, vicariously commit suicide in allowing Tony to die? These are questions that Wright leaves up in the air in order to focus on Fowler's feelings about Mrs. Blake.

Part Three, "Attack," describes the working out of Fowler's unconscious feelings—the emergence of long suppressed emotions which he has been dreading. As "Attack" opens Fowler still seethes with resentment at Mrs. Blake's wayward behavior, but nonetheless arranges to take her to dinner. When the hour arrives for him to call on her, however, he discovers that she has gone out. She leaves word for him to meet her at a bar—and there he meets several of her friends. It is clear from the start that Fowler and Mrs. Blake are worlds apart socially. Later she tells him when they are alone that it would be impossible for her to marry him, that they are too different. Fowler protests that she might at least attempt to know him better, but the question is left open. Later in her apartment the phone rings again and Fowler leaves her talking to another man. Boiling with hatred and jealousy, Fowler now sends her a note requesting that she release him from any promises he had made to her. He realizes now that they are not really suited for one another. He slips the note under her door and returns to his apartment. Some time later the phone rings again but when Fowler lifts the receiver there is no answer. Shortly thereafter Mrs. Blake appears at his door clothed only in her housecoat. She wants to know the reason for his strange behavior—his on again off again attitude toward her. They have a fierce argument in which Fowler admits that he was alone naked on the balcony with Tony, and Mrs. Blake admits that she had suspected him all along and that it was she who had been telephoning him. Each of them admits ruefully his complicity in Tony's death—and both again become somewhat reconciled to one another. Then the phone begins to ring in Mrs. Blake's apartment. She rises to answer it, but Fowler begs her not to go. She insists—and Fowler in a mountain of rage stabs away at her again and again with a butcher knife. Afterwards he dresses and goes down to the police station to report his crime. He remembers now a fantasy he had repressed as a child that his mother reprimanded him for stabbing a stuffed doll. The doll, he told himself, represented his mother. He realizes in the police station that that fantasy stemmed from a real memory in his childhood when he drew a picture of a dead doll with colored pencils and imagined that he had drawn a picture of his mother. When the police ask him why he committed the crime, he cannot answer. How could he tell them that his real motives derive from a childhood fantasy?

In closing the book as he does, one feels that Wright has somehow made short shrift of all the problems he had been so laboriously posing throughout the novel. It is as if he were saying that all things in life—human behavior, ethics, values, responsibilities—are at the mercy of unconscious passions, and that the unconscious will have its way regardless of man's efforts to solve his problems rationally. Although such psychological determinism may have its validity,

Wright does not give it much artistic support in his novel. First of all his main character has neither the stature nor the potential strength to put up the good fight with his irrational passions. He is enslaved from the very beginning—but unlike Cross Damon or Bigger Thomas he does not become even momentarily freed by his acts of violence. In fact, despite the color of his skin and his relatively high social position, Fowler reminds one of nothing so much as Wright's broken and humiliated southern Negroes. Like them Fowler is forced outside of life (in Fowler's case Longevity Life) and made a despairing, frustrated onlooker of activities in which he is unable to participate. And like them too, he is a living repository of fear, shame, and concealed hate that he is unable to vent properly.

But if Fowler is too weak a character to carry the burden of Wright's ideas, so is the narrative context in which Wright places him. As has been already pointed out, the chain of coincidences in Fowler's life leaves the reader somewhat incredulous. That Fowler should live next to a boy whose experiences so resemble his own is astounding to say the least. That Fowler should fall in love with a woman whose actual behavior so corresponds to that of his mother is going too far. This is not to say that some people do not project repressed feelings onto others in order to avoid the truth about themselves. The real problem is that there is no actual projecting. Tony *is* Fowler as a little boy, and Mrs. Blake *is* Fowler's mother. Surely the reader has the right to ask that they be different in some ways in order to point up perhaps all the better the irrationality of Fowler's passions.

These weaknesses of plot and characterization lead to others even more flagrant. Fowler's self-recognition, his insights into himself, come far too precipitously to lend credence to Wright's resolution. Moreover, because they are so obvious, they appear facile and, to make matters even worse, Wright phrases them in

psychoanalytical jargon. And possibly just as disturbing are the sudden changes in prose style which presumably are intended to reflect Fowler's newly acquired self-knowledge. But these transitions are jarring
and feel almost as "forced" as Wright's narrative.
From a tense, terse, almost reportorial account of the
murder Wright reverts to Fowler's childhood memories:

> he was looking in the mirror to see how bad he was,
> for his mother had said: "Go and look in the mirror
> at yourself and see how bad you are!" And he was look-
> ing at his face and the face he saw was his own and
> it wasn't bad . . . His mother had lied to him. He
> hadn't changed; he could see no bad in his face.[15]

In the final analysis *Savage Holiday* must be ac-
counted an artistic failure. One cannot escape the
feeling that Wright suddenly discovered himself
bored with the novel as a vehicle for his ideas—so he
rushed his plot to an unnatural conclusion. In any
event, for the next few years, Wright appears to be
more successful in translating his views into his semi-
journalistic studies of Asia and Africa. When he returned to the novel in 1957, it would be to retell the
story of the Negro boy in the racist South.

Social Freudianism
The Long Dream

When Richard Wright planned *The Long Dream* he evidently foresaw it as the first in a series of books dwelling on the life and career of Fishbelly Tucker, a Mississippi Negro boy who goes to live in France.[1] The autobiographical resemblances between the author and his protagonist are not however confined to mere geography. In many respects the psychic lives of the two appear to be very close—not to mention the fact that they both seem to have shared almost identical traumatic experiences. A reading of *Black Boy* alongside *The Long Dream* is instructive in this regard. Both Wright and Fishbelly, for example, at the age of six discover that their fathers are having illicit relations with women. Both boys have dreadful fears of being abandoned by their mothers; indeed Fishbelly has a dream not unlike the nightmares the four-year-old Wright suffered in the opening pages of *Black Boy*. Both boys do not come into any real contact with the brutality of the white world until their adolescent years, a fact which may account for their singular independence of spirit and defiance of caste ordinances. As a result both Fishbelly and Wright come to the conclusion that they are unable to accept the traditions and values of either white world or black, and must therefore seek the meaning of their lives in a different environment. In *The Long Dream* and *Black Boy* critical moments are described relating to the lynching and mutilation of a Negro bellhop who had been having an affair with a white prostitute. For both Fishbelly and Wright the death of the bellhop provides central insights into the connection between sex and caste. The Negro, they discover, who submits to white oppression is as much castrated psychologically as the bellhop is physically. Thus, for them the lynchings become symbolic of the roles they are expected to play in life. Finally, one is almost tempted to say that both Wright and Fishbelly share certain bourgeois backgrounds. Although Fishbelly is relatively affluent and Wright frequently destitute, both are reared in a middle-class milieu. (Wright's mother, aunts, and uncles, it will be remembered, were school teachers—and his grandparents owned property in Jackson.) Whatever else may be said of *Long Dream* it would be difficult to deny that Wright was once again reliving deeply embedded memories as a primary source for his new novel.

Whether or not Wright recognized himself in his characterization of Fishbelly is perhaps beside the point. What is, of course, relevant is what Wright aimed to do in his novel—and whether or not he succeeded. On the one hand he was intending to portray the growth of Fishbelly from childhood to manhood in psychosexual and social terms. On the other hand he was describing the complex sociological and political arrangements that exist between the white and Negro communities in a small southern town. To a very remarkable degree Wright achieved his purposes principally because he chose to focus his attention on one of the "leading" Negro families of Clintonville with whom the white power structure would have to negotiate. The very delicate interrelationship between subjective self-concepts and individual social and caste status has seldom been so successfully managed in any of Wright's other fiction. Perhaps the reason is that the Parisian Wright was now sufficiently detached from the violence of his Mississippi emotions to view his subject matter with greater objectivity. In any event there is a more careful consideration of character in relation to particular situation. Oddly, Wright, now twenty-nine years removed from Mississippi, provides his readers with a more tangible sense of time and place than in much of his earlier fiction. The metaphysical rebel at odds with a symbolically hostile and chaotic universe has been exchanged for a more human figure groping in a pragmatic American way with a very nearly impossible social dilemma. Ultimately, *The Long Dream* is a protest novel in the best sense of the term. Wright is not only protesting a caste system that keeps the Negro abjectly and humiliatingly dependent on the white world for his physical and economic survival but he is also crying out against the injustice that destroys his spirit, crushes his dignity. In a sense, too, the novel is didactic. It is intended to instruct readers once again that democracy for whites in the United States is not applicable to Negroes. In explaining the meaning of the title *The Long Dream* to a Paris reporter Wright suggested that his title was ironic "because Fishbelly's dream of identifying with white values can never be realized under existing circumstances."

Yet Wright never preaches in *Long Dream*—nor do his characters. Negroes and whites act according to their individual natures—which is not to say that all submit passively to their condition. Nonetheless nobody makes noble speeches for Negro freedom, nobody is converted, and action for the most part proceeds from character—rather than being imposed from without. Hence, there is a considerable honesty about this novel which is hard to gainsay. But there are awkward moments. Some of Wright's southern whites do not always sound authentic. The words they sometimes use are too "bookish" or stylized. It is as if Wright, like his Negroes, can never be at ease with them—and thus as a result can never render them quite accurately. And Wright sometimes puts into the mouths of his Negro characters words and expressions that had gone out of date at just about the time he left permanently for France—"pitch a boogie woogie," "jive," "cool killer," "killer diller," and so on. These are unfortunate but do no irreparable damage to the book. For all its anachronisms *Long Dream* says something profoundly true about its characters and the quality of their lives. And this after all is what a novel is supposed to do.

In centering his novel around Fishbelly, Wright often manages to relate Fishbelly's psychic development to his growing awareness of his social role. Fishbelly's psychology is unfolded largely from the point of view of his sexual understanding and attitudes—and these, from the very beginning, are confused. In part, of course the confusion is the result of the tenuous, ambivalent feelings any small child would have toward his parents. In part, the confusion results from the contradictory sexual standards—prohibitive, yet titillating and permissive—of the American culture. And finally, the confusion is but one more result of the welter of psychological maladies attendant on being a Negro in America. Within this latter category, Wright attempts to show that the bourgeois Negro often overcompensates in sexual terms for what he regards as his social and psychological emasculation by the white world.

Wright begins this very delicate observation of Fishbelly's psyche at the opening of the novel when he describes a dream his protagonist has when he is only six years old. In the dream Rex Tucker (he had yet to acquire the sobriquet Fishbelly) fancies that a huge, menacing fish flings a baseball at him which becomes wedged between his teeth. Rex knows that "the fish had done to him what his papa did to fishes catching him on a hook and the fish was coming at him with gleaming red eyes and he tried to scream but could not." [2] The phallic significance of the fish, its identification with his father, and its threatening posture obviously reflect Fishbelly's unconscious castration fears. For Rex, a fish has also a feminine association. The morning following his dream he watches his mother cleaning a pail full of fish his father had caught the night before. The smell of the fish resembles vaguely the smell of his mother's body and white fish bladders which his father teaches him to blow up into the dimensions of a balloon remind him of the inflated belly of a pregnant woman. Rex insists on calling the bladders bellies and this so amuses his friends that they thereupon call him Fishbelly—a name that was to stay with him all his life. The name has, of course, symbolic significance as well. It not only suggests a sexual confusion of masculine and feminine attributes in Fishbelly's character, but indicates that this confusion has its counterpart in Fishbelly's social outlook as well. Because he is brought up in the American culture, Fishbelly dreams the same dreams as the white world. But it is the white belly of the woman that symbolises his castration and he must live with this terror as part of his dream.

The first section of Wright's novel is called "Daydreams and Nightdreams" and shifts back and forth between Fishbelly's day-to-day life, his fantasies, his illusions, his values, his relationships to friends and family and the great world beyond—and unconscious dreams and desires that are conveyed in italicized stream-of-consciousness prose. "Daydreams and Nightdreams" constitutes nearly half the book and takes Fishbelly through his early adolescent years. It is episodic in content and comprises the chief events in Fishbelly's life as a child and youth. Part One ends with Fishbelly's induction into manhood and up to this point Wright skillfully selects his material and easily communicates Fishbelly's growth. The point of view is always Fishbelly's and the reader gradually comes to understand Fishbelly's world as that world slowly unfolds for Fishbelly. Expository and explanatory passages are kept to a minimum—there is none of the lyricism of some of Wright's early short stories—

and the story is told mostly in terms of dialogue. There is a naturalness to the prose—its cadences and vocabulary—when Wright confines himself to the talk of boys. The adults, with the exception of Fishbelly's father, introduce a jarring note. Wright, even at this late date, was perhaps at his surest when he dealt with youth.

It might be argued that in making his protagonist a member of the black bourgeoisie Wright was treading on dangerous new ground. Heretofore, it will be remembered, practically all of Wright's principal characters have been pariahs, peasants, proletarians, or dispossessed intellectuals. The one exception, Erskine Fowler of *Savage Holiday*, a member of the white bourgeoisie, was not altogether successfully realized. Yet, Wright, oddly enough, is in some ways in better control of Fishbelly than he was with a character like Bigger Thomas. This is not to say that *Long Dream* is a better novel than *Native Son* or that its impact is as great. The reason Fishbelly sounds more authentic is, paradoxically, that Wright is less ambitious in *Long Dream* than he had been in any of his other novels. There is no attempt here to fit Fishbelly into any political, metaphysical, or ideological pattern. He is non-intellectual, not overly social-conscious, and race-conscious only insofar as he recognizes that his needs and goals are frustrated by a caste system. He develops no far-reaching philosophy—although he subscribes vaguely to American concepts of equality and justice —and attempts to grapple with his problems on simple, practical grounds. He is not a sympathetic character in the sense that *Uncle Tom's Children* are, nor is he a monster or a "grotesque." Yet he arrives at certain social and psychological awarenesses as he goes along—which is to say *Long Dream* is in the long tradition of American novels which deal with search for identity and rebirth.

At critical moments in his life Fishbelly measures his growth and awareness according to his changing

attitudes towards his father, Tyree. Tyree is an undertaker, and since no white undertaker would deal with
Negro bodies in Clintonville, Tyree has a monopoly of
the Negro trade. In addition, he owns considerable
real estate—Negro slum tenements and a brothel. He
is therefore a significant force in the Negro community, a person with whom Clintonville white politicians and police often deal. For the young Fishbelly
he is an imposing figure, masterful and wise. He and
Fishbelly's mother, being both solid figures of the
Negro middle class, imbue Fishbelly with a respect for
the power of money and a sense of his social position
in relation to the poorer Negroes in the community.
When the six year old Fishbelly accidentally discovers
his father with another woman, he refuses to allow
himself to believe what he has seen—and the vision of
his father panting over his mistress is transformed into
an image of a locomotive in Fishbelly's dreams. From
time to time Wright reintroduces the dream motif of
the locomotive to convey Fishbelly's obsessive return
to this experience—and his unconscious will to reenact
his father's role. The initial impact of Fishbelly's
dream is rendered in a series of charging phrases sug-
gesting the erotic excitement—the terror, guilt, and
desire—of what Fishbelly had seen and felt:

> hurtling, sleek, black monsters whose stack pipes
> belched gobs of serpentine smoke, whose seething fire-
> boxes coughed out clouds of pink sparks, whose push-
> ing pistons sprayed jets of hissing steam—panting
> trains that roared yammeringly over far-flung, gleaming
> rails only to come to limp and convulsive halts—long,
> fearful trains that were hauled brutally forward by red-
> eyed locomotives that you loved watching as they (and
> you trembling!) crashed past (and you longing to run
> but finding your feet strangely glued to the ground!).[3]

Nearly every episode of Part One relates the themes
of race and sex. Indeed, Wright is saying that this is
the acculturation process of Negro youth in the South.
One episode, for example, describes Fishbelly and his

friends savagely beating an effeminate boy who wants
to play baseball with them. After the boy departs
Fishbelly considers his brutality and wonders at its
intensity. Has it anything to do with his being a
Negro? On another occasion Fishbelly and his friends
argue about their origins. Are they African or American? On still another occasion Fishbelly and his friends
fly in fear from a white prostitute who accosts them in
the woods and offers to sell herself. Earlier on the
same day the boys are made to feel shame and self-
contempt as they are urged by white onlookers to hit
the "nigger-head" with a wooden ball at a fair they are
attending. But not all the scenes of Fishbelly's childhood and youth are so grim. There are moments of
high spirits and broad good humour. There are mud
ball fights in the fields after a spring rain. There are
adolescent pranks that Fishbelly and his friends play
on their elders. There are the tense moments at school
when the schoolmaster seeks to discover the owner of
a batch of pornographic postcards. And there is finally
the vicarious delight, the embarrassment, the incredu-
lity, and the bravado of Fishbelly and his friends when
they discover one of their number has lost his virgin-
ity. Yet even at these lighter moments the terror and
hatred they carry about with them are never far from
their consciousness—and rare is the occasion on which
some acid allusion is not made to their condition.

As has been said before, Fishbelly's most critical
insights often come in relationship to his father. The
terror Tyree displays at the news that a Negro boy
(who is later lynched) has been discovered with a
white prostitute represents for Fishbelly bitter, angry
disillusionment with his father's manhood. Tyree, of
course, knows that such an incident can set off a race
riot—but for Fishbelly, Tyree's reactions and the reactions of the Negro community are shameful and humiliating. Yet despite his sudden illuminating hatred
for his father, the twelve year old Fishbelly recognizes
that his father feels the same shame and hatred to-

ward other Negroes. Nonetheless, Fishbelly inwardly resolves that he could no more accept southern Negro attitudes than he could white. Fishbelly's new sense of alienation from his family and other Negroes reminds one of the young Wright of *Black Boy*:

> From that night on, he was intuitively certain that he had a winking glimpse of how black people looked to white people; he was beginning to look at his people through alien eyes and what he saw evoked in him a sense of distance between him and his people that baffled and worried him.[4]

Some years later Fishbelly gains from his father's behavior further insights into the utter helplessness of Negroes. Fishbelly and his friend, Tony, have been arrested for trespassing on a white man's property. Tyree comes to the jail to secure their release—and Fishbelly is humiliated by Tyree's abject fawning, sycophantic behavior before minor white police officials. Later Tyree tries to introduce him into the rites of manhood by taking him to a Negro brothel. (Tyree's purpose, in part, was to warn his son away from the allure of the white world—to prove to him that the Negro world has its wiles, its pleasures.) But Fishbelly has already undertaken his own private rites into manhood. Earlier that day, returning through the woods from the jail, Fishbelly stumbles across a stricken dog that had evidently been hit by a passing car on the highway. After some hesitation Fishbelly decides to put the dog out of its suffering. He finds a shard of glass and cuts the dog's throat; then he proceeds to sever the dog's stomach and very methodically take out all its organs. By so doing Fishbelly has somehow purged himself of his castration fears—the police had earlier teased him with a knife—and he is now ready to face the white man's world on his own terms.

"Days and Nights," Part Two of *Long Dream*, follows along more self-contained plot lines. There are more of the familiar Wright intrigues, conspiracies and counter-conspiracies as Fishbelly is now given the opportunity to observe firsthand the political, economic, and social workings of the caste system. He discovers himself more removed from the world of dreams and thrust violently into the nightmare world of reality. Hence, the education of Fishbelly Tucker undergoes a new and different phase. Heretofore Fishbelly's major preoccupations were with his feelings; now he has little time to consider his feelings; he is so occupied with the world's work. The tone and pace of Part Two change accordingly. The rambling, discursive air of "Daydreams" is transformed into something more concentrated and quickened. There is less dependence on dialogue and more on straight narration —always, of course, from Fishbelly's point of view. Because Fishbelly is now dealing more with the adult world, dialogue is less natural—and this, as has been already noted, is particularly true of white adults.

The most singular achievement of this section is not, however, Wright's facility in moving Fishbelly from a subjective world to an external world—but rather the very remarkable portrait of Tyree. Indeed, though it is obviously not Wright's intention, it is Tyree who runs away with the novel—and it is Tyree one remembers most vividly after one has finished the novel. It is doubly astonishing because there is very little in Wright's previous works to prepare the reader for Tyree. All of Wright's other major characters run to certain emotional, intellectual, or ideological types —but Tyree stands alone in Wright's fiction as a kind of heroic anti-hero, aware neither of his stature nor of his meanness. How explain him? Is he the father Wright would have liked? One can only guess that in portraying Tyree, Wright allowed his imagination free rein—and that Tyree in the course of events took hold of Wright's prose and diverted the principal emphasis away from his son.

If Tyree did indeed redirect the true course of the novel, it would not be inappropriate to his character. He is of such an ingenuous and cunning nature that one could scarcely expect to meet him without being deeply affected and considerably disturbed. He represents in some ways, one supposes, the survival of the fittest of the oppressed in a racist community. Fishbelly comes to know him better now than he did in the earlier portions of the novel because he goes to work for him. Tyree had wanted Fishbelly to finish school and go on to university, but Fishbelly had become so distracted by a love affair he was having with a near-white prostitute that he failed his examinations and quit school. Fishbelly has the ability to manipulate his father because he knows Tyree cherishes him and wants him to inherit the business. Tyree thus succumbs to Fishbelly's not-so-veiled threats that if Tyree insists he go back to school, he will leave home. Tyree is a hard-driving employer. He puts Fishbelly to work first as his rent collector in the slums. Fishbelly learns that his father is not only a rather heartless landlord, but that he works in collusion with the police in collecting graft from his brothels. Thus Tyree, whose survival depends on the favors of distant white masters, is as ruthless an exploiter of his people as any less subtle white supremacist. Wright is saying here that the black bourgeoisie in southern communities fattens itself on the misery of the Negro masses—and flourishes not despite, but because of the caste system. Tyree (and Fishbelly, too, to an extent) are willing tools of a corrupt and corrupting society. They do not particularly like the roles they play but recognize that they must accommodate themselves to the world as it is if they are to survive. Outwardly, Tyree is expected to convey the impression of the solid respected Negro leader, Christian and charitable, moderately independent, but properly deferential to "white folks." Yet Tyree knows that to enact this part successfully he must be more clever than his white rulers, who use him ruthlessly, and hypocritical and deceptive toward the Negroes of the community, whose best interests he is supposed to represent.

If, however, Tyree were simply this kind of Negro

leader he would be interesting, but not after all, terribly different from some of his white counterparts, who are hacks or instruments of powerful political or business interests. What makes Tyree somewhat different is the almost intuitive artistry he employs in keeping all the contending interests for his soul, his money, his time, and his affections nicely in balance. He maintains a wife and home and is apparently a large contributor to one of the Negro churches. He maintains as well a rather splendid mistress who is obviously very loyal to him. He is an unsentimental, shrewd, relentless businessman as regards his real estate properties—yet he is capable of assuming pious, saccharine solemnities in the conduct of his undertaking establishment. He can be calculating and predatory (in Part One he prepares to seduce the mother of a boy who has just been lynched); at the same time he genuinely loves, perhaps adores, his son. Finally, he is capable of striking the most corrupt bargains with white civic authorities and yet remains deluded as to the innocence of his son.

Tyree's real character emerges as a result of a number of dramatic events. One Fourth of July an enormous Negro dancehall—a rendezvous for Negro prostitutes—burns to the ground, killing forty-five persons within. (Actually Wright may have been remembering the burning of a Negro dancehall in Natchez in June, 1940.) One of the victims is Gladys, Fishbelly's mistress, but Fishbelly, nonetheless, musters up sufficient presence of mind to petition the police chief, Cantley, to allow his father to bury the corpses. Fishbelly wonders later why his father does not appear overjoyed at what Fishbelly regards as a business coup. It soon develops that Tyree is a secret partner of Dr. Bruce, the owner of the dancehall—and Tyree fears that it will look as if he is profiting as much by his customers' deaths as he did when they were alive. (Fishbelly, too, belatedly recognizes that the money he was paying Gladys for her affections was in actuality going right back to him, since Gladys had to use the dancehall as her place of business.) Tyree's real fear, however, is that he will be arrested and sent to jail for negligence or manslaughter in overlooking the fire regulations. Since he could not have done this without the concurrence of the police, Tyree pleads with Cantley that the white civic authorities spare him. But the scandal of the fire is too big to cover up—and Cantley knows somebody has to serve as scapegoat. Cantley, meanwhile, is afraid (not without justification) that Tyree, if he is sent to jail, will implicate him in other municipal scandals. The confrontation between Tyree and Cantley—to which Fishbelly and Dr. Bruce are witness—is one of the best scenes in the novel. Tyree is alternately abject, fawning, flattering, smiling, sobbing, humble, grateful, and apologetic—and in his own strange way vaguely threatening. Underneath all Tyree's obsequious pleading one feels a towering passion, a hatred so intense of his white enemies that it would frighten Tyree himself were he fully aware of his feelings. Yet despite this Tyree continues to play shrewdly on all the misconceptions and preconceptions southern racists have about Negroes. Dr. Bruce and Fishbelly are astounded at his performance—and he nearly succeeds in convincing the suspicious and distrustful Cantley that he would not betray him. When Tyree decides that his erstwhile white collaborators will not help him, he determines he will drag as many of them down with him as he can. He will not be destroyed so easily by the whites whom he has hated all along. Despite the immense danger to his life, Tyree sends a batch of cancelled checks to a reform politician implicating Cantley in some of Tyree's nefarious enterprises. Cantley manages to intercept the evidence and later traps Tyree in one of his brothels and kills him. Tyree's death places the onus of all his business activities on Fishbelly's young shoulders (he is only seventeen). Yet for Fishbelly the great heritage of Tyree is not his

business, but his example. Despite his cunning, his
dishonesty, his shame, his self-contempt, Tyree was a
man. His courage in fighting his white oppressors
proved he was a man—and in death Fishbelly found
his father.

In addition to Tyree, there are a number of other
fine portraits in "Days and Nights." There is, for example, Gladys, Fishbelly's girl, whose complexion is so
fair that she could "pass." Yet it never occurs to her
that she should. Nor is she at all outraged at southern
racism that brands her inferior—or the fortunes that
compelled her to enter her profession. Wright here
implies that her status in the community is the most
precarious of all persons inasmuch as she belongs neither to the white nor the black—and she is thus con-
sidered fair game for the predatory males of both
races. Fishbelly is exasperated at her racial indifference, yet he chooses her initially because she looks so
white. Indeed, Wright describes a vivid scene in which
a rejected dark-skinned prostitute insults and sneers at
Fishbelly and his friends for passing her up because of
her color. She is right, too. White racial standards
have infected the Negro community.

Besides Gladys and her prostitute friends, Fishbelly
meets a variety of Negro "types" in the tenements at
which he collects rents. They range in profession from
prostitutes, to working people, to a prissy retired
schoolmistress. Each is in his own way a "grotesque";
each has had something destroyed or stunted in him
because he is impoverished and a Negro. Wright describes Fishbelly's encounters with them as he tries to
collect their rent. Here the reader no longer finds any
of Wright's idealization or romanticizing of the southern Negro poor. Uncle Tom's children are as sick in
spirit as the fattened bourgeoisie. And they are as
obsessed with "race" as the worst of their white masters.

If Wright's whites still tend more toward stereotype, it is perhaps worthy of note that they are some-

what more human. Even Cantley, the villain of the piece, cries out in his own agony at one juncture, "Oh, goddamn this sonofabitching world! Goddamn everything!" But Wright uses white characters in the novel not simply to illustrate realities of the power arrangement between the white and black communities, but to reveal how racism implicitly dominates the protocol and mores of personal relationships, how speech patterns vary, how tones and gestures change whenever the races confront one another. Tyree, for example, never looks a white man in the eye. He adopts a whining air. He stands a little hunched with a half smile on his face. When the white man calls, Tyree must be ready to drop anything in order to meet him. (Early in the book Tyree calls a halt to a promised liaison with one of his ladies because Cantley has notified him that he wishes to see him.) On the other hand Tyree may never petition the police chief or the mayor when he encounters a problem, but must instead await a message from them before he proceeds with any new undertaking. Tyree's success, of course, depends in large part on how well he debases himself in white men's eyes. Fishbelly (like the young Wright) could never play-act the role of the grateful minstrel so well as Tyree. As a result Fishbelly's defiance somehow conveys itself to whites and they can never really be sure of him. This is to be Fishbelly's dilemma in the third and final section of the book, "Waking Dream."

"Waking Dream" derives its title from Shakespeare's *Cymbeline*:

> The dream's here still: even when I wake it is
> Without me, as within me: not imagined.

Hence Fishbelly, now aroused to new levels of reality by the death of his father, the onus of his new responsibilities and his awareness of the helplessness of being a Negro, nonetheless dreams the dream of freedom and human dignity. He is partially inspired by Tyree's blistering hatred of whites that lives on evidently after his death. The plot develops that Tyree did not surrender all the evidence damning Cantley, after all. More cancelled checks with Cantley's signature on them come secretly into Fishbelly's possession. He carefully conceals them in his room and pretends he knows nothing. Cantley (now retired from the police force, but still evidently a major power behind the scenes) suspects Fishbelly. Fishbelly is arrested on a trumped-up charge and kept in prison for two years. Cantley hopes that Fishbelly, in that time, will reveal what he knows—if indeed he knows anything. But Fishbelly resolves that he would rather rot in jail than trust Cantley. While in jail Fishbelly receives letters from his old school chums who are now in the army in France. They write that France is free of racism, Parisian women are fine, and how they loathe the thought of going back to Mississippi. When Fishbelly is finally released, he determines to go to France. Cantley asks him to take up where his father left off—that is to collect graft—and Fishbelly pretends to accede. But actually he steals out of town at the first opportunity. The novel ends with Fishbelly seated aboard a plane bound for Paris. He has mailed back Cantley's checks to a reform politician in Clintonville. Meanwhile Fishbelly hopes that perhaps in Paris he will find the realization of his long dream.

"Waking Dream" suffers in comparison with the other two sections of Wright's novel. It is almost painfully evident that Wright does not know quite how to end his book—and so he ends it quickly. Fishbelly's two years in prison are capsuled into a few pages; Cantley's sudden decision to trust Fishbelly (he gives Fishbelly three thousand dollars as his share of unpaid bribe money when Fishbelly is released from prison), and Fishbelly's sudden flight and escape from Clintonville are rather implausible, given the circumstances. All told, "Waking Dream" feels as if it were grafted onto the novel by another author. With the

exception of one lengthy passage describing Clintonville's mass funeral for its forty-five burned victims,
Wright's "feel" for social detail and concrete physical
setting seems now rather perfunctory. Nor does the
story line really even allow Wright to explore the
complexities of Fishbelly's new personality. To be
sure, Fishbelly emerges strengthened, hardened, fixed,
as it were, in his purpose—but these appear as surface
manifestations. The "underground man" of Part One
is as missing as the social realities of Part Two.

But Wright does attempt to complete the broad
spectrum of Negro society that he presented in "Days
and Nights." Perhaps more important than even the
black bourgeoisie in organizing and directing the
southern Negro community is the Negro church. Indeed, the church appears to be, in some rural areas,
the only institution that serves as a repository and
outlet for southern Negro political and social views.
Clintonville is not that primitive a community; nonetheless its Negro section is made up of persons perhaps
only one or two generations removed from the soil.
Hence, churches still retain a powerful influence in
shaping Negro opinion. It is significant in *Long
Dream* that Tyree, just before the police killed him,
had arranged for the religious services for the persons
who had died in his dancehall. Ironically, Tyree now
shares the same funeral service as his victims. Thus the
black bourgeoisie and certain components of the
Negro church partake of an identity of interests in
diverting the natural discontent and bitterness of the
Negro community. Reverend Ragland makes clear to
the mourners that the causes of their suffering are not
white men or a corrupt economic and political system
—but God, and He works in mysterious ways:

> Who dares say how many of us'll be here a year from
> now? Your future's in the hollow of Gawd's Hands!
> Now, there's men in this town who say that they run
> it! . . . The men who run this town can be white as
> snow, but *we* know who's boss! GAWD'S THE BOSS! And

He's more powerful than the president, the governor, the mayor, the chief of police.[5]

The Reverend's sermon represents some of the best writing in the book. It is curious that Wright, the atheist, could still after so many years render so well the feel of a Negro church service.

But when Wright removes Fishbelly from the Negro world, and sends him first to jail and then on his way to France to seek his dream, something "untrue" happens to the book. It is difficult to say why. Clearly everything Wright has said up to this point, he has said well. He has created real-life characters whose experiences are believable. He has proved that the world they live in not only exploits them shamelessly but debilitates them spiritually. He has portrayed, with refreshing candor the day-to-day life of a middle-sized southern urban Negro community, and has revealed that the sickness that dwells therein has its roots in a variety of grounds—Freudian, economic, political, and cultural. In this sense Wright's objectivity accounts for the lessened impact of *Long Dream* in comparison with some of his other novels. Neither Fishbelly nor his father is a "sympathetic" character. Each has become too corrupted by white bourgeois values and a kind of reverse racism. Both recognize ruefully that a system of ethics is a luxury they cannot afford. (At one juncture Fishbelly schemes to bribe an illiterate Negro ex-convict to take the blame for Tyree's criminal negligence.) Mere physical survival then appears to be the immediate goal, aim, and value in all Negro lives. But physical survival in a concrete, known setting is preferable, artistically at least, to idealistic theorizing and dreaming in an unknown environment. The most kindly disposed reader is likely to demand that any dream, however long, be related to an authentic environment. And Fishbelly's removal from that environment somehow alloys the dream. It is of course a cruel paradox because Fishbelly's dream of dignity and freedom can never be realized in a racist Mississippi milieu either. It is perhaps this same paradox that confounded Fishbelly's author thousands of miles away in Paris. And it is doubtless because he could not resolve it that Richard Wright seldom achieved his fullest measure of artistic promise.

Notes

2—The Fractured Personality
Black Boy; 12 Million Black Voices

1. *Black Boy* (New York, 1945), p. 40.
2. *Ibid.*, p. 127.
3. The speech is included in *White Man, Listen!* (1956).
4. *12 Million Black Voices* (New York, 1941) pp. 146–47.
5. *Ibid.*, p. 61. 6. *Ibid.*, p. 118. 7. *Ibid.*, p. 123.
8. *Ibid.*, p. 27. 9. *Ibid.*, p. 32.

3—The Fractured Personality
Black Power; Pagan Spain

1. George Padmore, the London-based African historian, was at this time an aide and close advisor of Nkrumah.
2. *Black Power* (New York, 1954), pp. xii, xv.
3. *Ibid.*, p. 4. 4. *Ibid.*, p. 66.
5. *Ibid.*, p. 171. 6. *Ibid.*, p. 345.
7. *Ibid.*, p. 348. 8. *Ibid.*, p. 158. 9. *Ibid.*, pp. 324–25.
10. *Pagan Spain* (New York, 1957), p. 151.
11. *Ibid.*, p. 116. 12. *Ibid.*, p. 98. 13. *Ibid.*, p. 61.
14. *Ibid.*, p. 88. 15. *Ibid.*, pp. 187–88. 16. *Ibid.*, p. 193.
17. *Ibid.*, p. 17. 18. *Ibid.*, p. 138.

4—The Shattered Civilization
The Color Curtain; White Man, Listen!

1. *The Color Curtain* (Cleveland and New York, 1956), pp. 11, 14.
2. *Ibid.*, p. 14. 3. *Ibid.*, p. 140.

4. Quoted in Ollie Harrington's article, "The Last Days of Richard Wright," *Ebony*, XVII (February 1961), p. 84.

5. *Color Curtain*, p. 166.

6. *Ibid.*, p. 165.

7. *Ibid.*, p. 200.

5—The Short Stories:
Uncle Tom's Children; Eight Men

1. The edition I use in this chapter was published as the seventh printing of Tower Books by World Publishing Company (New York and Cleveland, 1946).

2. See "The Art of Richard Wright's Short Stories" in *Quarterly Review of Literature*, I (Spring 1944), 198–211.

3. *Uncle Tom's Children*, pp. 64–65.

4. *Ibid.*, pp. 148–49. 5. *Ibid.*, p. 135. 6. *Ibid.*, pp. 210–11.

7. *Ibid.*, p. 201. 8. *Ibid.*, p. 250.

9. The first edition of *Eight Men* was published by World (New York and Cleveland, 1961). The edition which I use for this chapter was published later the same year by Avon, New York, in paper cover.

10. *Eight Men*, p. 34.

11. *Ibid.*, p. 68. 12. *Ibid.*, p. 50.

13. "The Man Who Killed A. Shadow," Zero I (Spring 1949), 45–53.

14. *Ibid.*, p. 100.

15. Neither "Man of All Work" nor "Man, God Ain't Like That" had been published prior to *Eight Men*. It is therefore difficult to date either but the latter sounds as if it may have been written after Wright's return from the Gold Coast in the fall of 1953.

16. *Ibid.*, p. 71.

17. *Ibid.*

6—Foreshadowings: Lawd Today

1. *Lawd Today* (New York, 1963), p. 30.

2. *Ibid.*, p. 32. 3. *Ibid.*, pp. 153–54. 4. *Ibid.*, p. 86.

5. *Ibid.*, p. 48. 6. *Ibid.*, pp. 24–25. 7. *Ibid.*, p. 125.

7—Revolution: Native Son

1. *Native Son* (New York, 1940), p. 50.
2. *Ibid.,* p. 7. 3. *Ibid.,* p. 203. 4. *Ibid.,* p. 358.
5. *Ibid.,* pp. 335–36. 6. *Ibid.,* p. 97.
7. Albert Camus, *The Rebel* (New York, Vintage, 1956) pp. 48–49.
8. *Ibid.,* p. 60.

8—The Existential Freud
    The Outsider; Savage Holiday

1. *The Outsider* (New York, 1953).
2. *Ibid.,* p. 209.
3. "Black Boy in France," *Ebony,* VIII(July 1953), p. 41.
4. *The Outsider,* p. 109. The lines are from Hart Crane's "Legend," and precede the text of "Dream."
5. *Ibid.,* p. 109. Compare with Sartre's "man is a useless passion," quoted in *Existentialism from Dostoevsky to Sartre,* ed. Walter Kaufman (Cleveland, 1956), p. 47.
6. *Ibid.,* p. 173. 7. *Ibid.,* p. 183. 8. *Ibid.,* p. 276.
9. *Ibid.,* p. 333. 10. *Ibid.,* p. 405. 11. *Ibid.,* p. 404.
12. *Savage Holiday* (New York, Avon, 1954), p. 38.
13. *Ibid.,* p. 29. 14. *Ibid.,* p. 30. 15. *Ibid.,* p. 214.

9—Social Freudianism: The Long Dream

1. *The Long Dream* (Garden City, 1958).
2. *Ibid.,* p. 10. 3. *Ibid.,* p. 27.
4. *Ibid.,* p. 67. 5. *Ibid.,* p. 327.

Selected Bibliography

FICTION

Uncle Tom's Children: five long stories. New York, 1940.
Native Son. New York, 1940.
Native Son, the Biography of a Young American. A Play in Ten Scenes. By Paul Green and Richard Wright. New York, 1941.
The Outsider. New York, 1953.
Savage Holiday. New York, 1954.
The Long Dream. New York, 1958.
Eight Men. Cleveland and New York, 1961.
Lawd Today. New York, 1963.
"Five Episodes" (from an unfinished novel), in Herbert Hill ed., *Soon One Morning,* New York, 1963.

NONFICTION

12 Million Black Voices: A Folk History of the Negro in the United States. Photo direction by Edwin Rosskam. New York, 1941.
Black Boy: A Record of Childhood and Youth. New York, 1945.
Black Power: A Record of Reactions in a Land of Pathos. New York, 1954.
The Color Curtain: A Report on the Bandung Conference. Cleveland and New York, 1956.
Pagan Spain. New York, 1956.
White Man, Listen! New York, 1957.

The only full length biography to date is *Richard Wright,* New York, 1968, by Constance Webb.

For a complete bibliography of Wright's published works, see Fabre, Michel and Edward Margolies, "Richard Wright (1908–1960)," *Bulletin of Bibliography,* XXIV (January–April, 1965), 131–33, 137.

Index